We took the rhymes and beats from childhood.

We grew up on them.

We grew with them.

We immortalized them.

The words branded themselves into our lives.

Like the artists within we don't apologize and we don't explain our actions.

Let the integrity of the collaboration stand uncluttered.

LOVE IT.

HATE IT.

COLLECT IT.

DEBATE IT.

We are proud to generate the first of many works of heart and mind that demand we remember and know, not just consume.

We are what we challenge.

The challenge is a process.

The process is this collaboration.

SBP

Hip Hop Immortals Volume 1 The Remix

Written by Bonz Malone
for Sock Bandit Productions

Edited by Nichole Beattie
for Sock Bandit Productions

Co-Edited by DJ Lindy
for Sock Bandit Productions

Sock Bandit Productions

I know what you're thinking, 'Oh God, not another glossy, flossy, rap pictorial written in a condescending tone

by some self-proclaimed "authority" fresh out of Yale.' Wrong! I wrote this in jail, contracted by Sock Bandit to

lay down a track to the images they've captured as Hip-Hop's 100 Immortals. Am I a self-proclaimed authority?

I don't have to be. All I got to do is have the ballz to sign my name, the same way I did on the trains and that

makes me a fan. What makes me sure that you'll be beefing over the names that were encoded in the volume?

Because it was written that way. The job of the fan is to get emotional over the beats, the rhymes, the pictures,

and the coverage. It's part of the work detail to send letters threatening writers and editors, because you love

the universal culture and appreciate the art. If this were not true, then you would not pick up this joint in the inter-

est of making sure we got it tight, right?   No doubt, you'll discover some names that are not entered. There

are some who still have to earn their burn to be called "starz," let alone "immortals." In any case, I must report

what I see and not what I would like to see or think I should see. My objective henceforth, is neither interpreta-

tion nor advocacy, but description. Wish me luck! This may piss you off, I hope it does! I'm a fan, too. It's my job

to do that and to make you really happy with the characterizations of the heroes that did.

I may not be famous, but my image is. I cast a universal shadow of the consummate B-Boy. I'm a product of

urban animation, better known as hip-hop; the most alluring and misrepresented culture this side of the grave.

No, not this *cosmoplatinium* crap-rap that equates to junk bonds, sold to out-of-vogue suckers who regret not

having a ghetto of their own to culturize, so they plagiarize. You think you know the distant world from which I

speak, then close your eyes and peep this.....Once upon a time, in a land far-far away, when gangz ran Gotham

and the halls of injustice were covered with the names of the fallen, there emerged a king whose power trans-

formed violence into valiance. Like sweet music, his dream of street solidarity captured the minds and hearts of his sworn enemies, who soon became loyal and gallant knights of his round ideology. Together they schooled a paradigm of war's alternative to society's most wan

outlaws, making them well needed ghetto superheroes for what seemed then as the bold, new world. A multicultural utopia where graffiti artisticrats painted suns

which created moods and characters that rhymes brought to life. An enchanting pastime, enjoyed with assorted confederates, when free lunch was served in the

schoolyard. BVDs and stitched Lees were the acceptable uniform for upstarts like myself. Coveted were the long navy blazers, tooth-brushed Playboys worn exclusiv

by *blackiavellianz* who maintained perfect 360 degree wave patterns that were concealed under iron-creased, spitfire kangols. These were the first born sons of the u

ed kingdom of heroes; men of request who needed no introduction. Their lives validated a style that connected to status symbols of immeasurable power. These f

mer war criminals stomped a mudhole into my memory as I fathom their elegant strolls down Tuph St.™ in soft British loafuhz. They had graduated from the schoo

hardrockz and were lionized as valedictorians of non-violence. Knowledge of self was the chapter that was being written back then from a book that would be hanc

down to children of the ghetto on how to achieve greatness. This is that book.

Before we begin, I'd like to explain the meaning of the word, *forward*. It simply means: advance. Simpler said than done many times when lyrics seemingly set us ba

fifty years. Rap, as a business, is more about making money than it is about making a difference. At least to the corporate bottom line anyway. Those rare artists w

achieve "Immortal Status" have always understood themselves, the fan, the payola, and the difference between Rap The Industry and Hip-Hop the culture that chang

General Market. When negative publicity makes headlines over the art, the fan blames the media or the conglomerate. They're only partially right. The effectiveness

government propaganda increases when dispensed under the guise of independent and impartial judgement. The greater the prestige and visibility of the individuals

nstitutions dispensing the propaganda, the greater its effect. As an educated fan on this subject, the blame should not be totally on the tool used. The challengers a

...mies of censorship(i.e. rap artists) are equally dependent on propaganda for making their case, gathering support, and recruiting followers towards the ideologies

...advocate. Because of this, each artist and aspiring one, is responsible and should be held accountable for advancing all the areas we influence; without exception,

...at times, with questionable intention. Don't expect a network anchor or journalist for a daily rag to get this point with clarity. To them, like our parents, bitches, nig-

...hoes,, and faggots aren't nice words. They don't understand that that's the way we give "shout outs" to our peeps. Can you dig it? Maybe not. Maybe they have

...origin of reference on this subject that doesn't greatly consist of the present day misinterpretations of immortality? We do! By digging in the crates for old conven-

...records with *Charlie Chase vs. Grand Wizard Theodore* or "The Adventures of Grand Master Flash on the Wheels of Steel," purchasing graffiti magazines and wit-

...sing how Aerosol Art has sprayed all across the world, watching the legendary DMC World Supremacy DJ battles on home video, or attending the Zulu Nation and

...k Steady Anniversaries held each year; they'll see for themselves what every name mentioned in this book wanted to behold and then become...not a Bitch, a Nigga,

...be, or a Faggot—just famous! I recently read a profound comment made by one of the dispensers, Michael Bloomberg, in the March issue of *Fast Company*. He

...ed,

...e learned that change is always evolutionary and is virtually never revolutionary."This best describes the reason why I wrote this book. Hip-hop is the only great thing

...was created suddenly. I wish Kool Herc would have put a patent on it. His kids would be as rich as Rap is.

The End,
by Bonz Malone

I know what you're thinking. 'Oh God, not another glossy, flossy, rap picto[rial-written in a] condescending tone by some self-proclaimed, 'Authority', fresh out of Yale'. Wrong! I wrote this jailz contracted by Immortal Brands to lay down a track to the images they've captured as Hip-Hop Immortals. Am I a self-proclaimed authority...

(overlapping large type, partially legible:) faggots ballz gangz out-laws exclusively by black-British Hip-Hop challengers and Aerosol Art Rapist

...in a land far-far-away, when ... ran gotham and the halls of injustice were covered with sweet music ... there emerged a king whose power transformed violence into laws ... worn enemies, who soon became loyal and gallant knights of its round ideology. Together ... a paradigm of war's alternative to society's most wanted ... making them well ... graffiti art students for what seemed then as the bo[ld] new world. A multi-cultural utopia where graffiti artists ... painted sunsets which created ... enchanting pastime ... old school ... They had graduated from the school of hardrockz and lionized as valedictorians of non-violence. Knowledge of self was the chapter that was being written back then, from a book that would be handed down to children of the ghetto on how to achieve greatness. This is that book.

Before we begin, I'd like to explain the meaning of the word, Forward. It simply means, "Advance." Simply ... Rap as a business is more about making money than ... bottom line anyway. Those rare artists who achieve ... have always understood them-selves ... Rap and the difference between Rap, the business and ...

...of censorship(i.e.: Rap Artists), are equally dependen[t] ... be held accountable for advertising ... Don't expose ... parents ... understand that that's the way we give ...no origin of reference on this ... interpretations of immortality? We do! By diggi[ng] ... Grand Wizard Theodore, or The Adventure[s] ... that survived across the world, the ...this is the reason why I wrote this book. Hip-Hop is truly great music that was created suddenly. ...would have put a period on it...

Hip Hop

Art Direction And Design/Giovanni C. Russo/No 11

Immortals

ALL HAIL THE KING & CREATOR OF G-FUNK. NEARLY EVERY SINGLE PROFESSIONAL ENDEAVOR THAT DR. DRE HAS EMBARKED ON HAS MARKED HIM AS AN IMMORTAL. WHATEVER—AND WHOMEVER—HE TOUCHES TURNS TO GOLD. A FORMER MEMBER OF THE WORLD CLASS WRECKIN' CRU AND N.W.A. ANDRE YOUNG LEFT THE LATTER IN 1992 TO FORM DEATH ROW RECORDS WITH SUGE KNIGHT. THESE TWO TITANS SUBSEQUENTLY WENT ON TO RULE THE MUSIC INDUSTRY FOR THE NEXT FOUR YEARS. ALWAYS TEN STEPS AHEAD OF THE GAME, DRE—HINTING AT THE DEATH OF GANGSTA RAP—DEPARTED DEATH ROW IN 1996 TO FORM AFTERMATH RECORDS. IN 1997 DRE SIGNED AN UNKNOWN MC FROM DETROIT, MICHIGAN AND TWO YEARS LATER A STAR WAS BORN WITH THE 1999 DEBUT OF EMINEM. THE DOCTOR'S EXTRAORDINARY PRODUCTION TECHNIQUE TRADEMARKED A SLOW-ROLLIN' SOUND FOR EVERYTHING THAT HAD CHROME RIMS ACROSS AMERICA. HIS MUSICAL GENIUS HAS INFECTED OVER FIFTY LPS AND OVER TEN SOUNDTRACKS INCLUDING: 2PAC'S *ALL EYEZ ON ME*, SNOOP DOGG'S *DOGGYSTYLE*, ICE CUBE'S *WAR & PEACE VOL. 2*, N.W.A.'S *STRAIGHT OUTTA COMPTON* AND *100 MILES AND RUNNIN'*, AND DRE'S VERY OWN LEGENDARY SOLO DEBUT *THE CHRONIC*. BECAUSE OF HIS SUPERIOR SKILLS AS A PRODUCER AND HIS INCREDIBLE EYE FOR TALENT, DRE HAS CONSISTENTLY REMAINED ON TOP, REFUSING TO GIVE UP THE THRONE TO ANYONE. COMPETITION ISN'T A GAME FOR THIS MAN, IT'S HIS BREAKFAST. HE'S AS SMALL AS TEXAS.

He is the man who put the 'ph' in Fat Tuesdays. A CEO, rapper, actor, and uncanny entrepreneur; Percy Miller was a true sleeper. Did you see this one coming? Did you know that No Limit was a record store before it was a label? And did you know that before his rap compilations *Down South Hustlers/West Coast Bad Boyz* entered the charts he had already sold a quarter of a million records without any distribution or a record deal? Master P signed with Priority Records for national distribution and every joint he's dropped that made noise has hit the Billboard chart! At the height of their production, the former record store was putting out 20-35 albums a month. With no publicity and foot-soldiers working street teams, Percy Miller made countless millions. No Limit expanded under Master P's vision, starting No Limit Films—the first hip-hop oriented straight-to-video company. Through shameless promotion No Limit made almost as much money, if not more, in the film industry as they had in the music end. He owns a gas station, a Foot Locker outlet, and lives behind gates across the yard from the former Governor of Louisiana! Percy's an inspiration—not just to the dirty south ballerz getting' caked out with white diamond frosting, but because he learned the secret to the American dream…ownership.

Master P

biz markie biz markie

Without question R
Premier court jester of
goofy lyrics and...

ticket in town two legenda...

Markie put on a show

Without question, Biz Markie is hip-hop's Premier Court Jester. But one look beyond his goofy lyrics and out-of-tune vocals and therein lies a superb **freestyler** whose comedic antics appealed to the masses but clever rhyme saying entrusted respect from the streets. Along with Roxanne Shante, Big Daddy Kane, and MC Shan, Biz was one of the first members of producer Marley Marl's renowned Juice Crew. *Goin' Off* was Biz Markie's 1988 debut which showcased the classic singles "Picking Boogers," "Vapors," and "Make the Music with Your Mouth, Biz." His superhuman beat-boxing on this album started a frenzy on the grapevine eventually thrusting Biz out of the underground and into a boom-box near you. In 1988 Biz was the hottest ticket in town. He'd step into the Roxy and Funhouse (two legendary NY clubs) clad in outrageous wigs and start whylin' on the mic, performing songs that would make you wet your pants. Almost as important as an MC's lyrical ability is his or her stage presence and when Biz Markie put on a show it was grade A, stand-up comedy… with a bumpin' beat. 1989 saw the release of his second album, *The Biz Never Sleeps,* which spawned one of hip-hop's most widely popular tunes, "Just A Friend"—an hysterical heart wrenching tale of Biz's quest for his true love who swears that the other dude in her life is just a friend until he walks in on them arranged in a compromising position in her college dorm-room. His third album, *I Need a Haircut* (1991), was plagued with legal problems surrounding the unauthorized sampling of Gilbert O'Sullivan's "Alone Again." The court demanded that the album be pulled from shelves and delivered a huge blow to the hip-hop industry when it ruled that all labels had to start clearing samples before releasing an album. Although his last album, *All Samples Cleared,* was released in 1993, Biz remained a fixture in the community popping up at shows here and there either as a DJ or guest entertainer. He may always be the designated **disco clown** but Biz Markie was completely down with hip-hop culture in every aspect: MC, DJ, dancer, and writer. Hip-hop is saved by guys like him. Pick up any of his albums and feel how chill rap was because of the Biz. It's virtually impossible to dislike the man or his music; it's rowdy combination of mad-comedy and human beats let us know that it is indeed true—nobody beats the Biz… for riz.

Nas

Born Nasir Jones in the infamous Queensbridge Housing projects of Queens, New York, Nasty Nas is one of the most talented MCs to ever bless a microphone. His raspy voice is simultaneously
powerful and subdued, rapping
compellingly of a grim life on the streets without glorifying violence or misogyny. *Illmatic* marked Nas as the second coming of
Jesus Christ… or at least his righteous predecessor, Rakim. Whether it's in his blood (his father is famed jazz trumpeter Olu Dara) or in the water in the QB Projects
(Mobb Deep, MC Shan, and Craig G all claim them as home) Nas is an incredibly gifted artist whose lyrical prose raised the bar for every MC to follow
him.

Super Busta Rhymes

Super Busta Rhymes

HIS RALLYING CALL, "WOO HA,"
SUPERHUMAN CARICATURE AN' [
DEEPER THAN THAT. HE IS ARGU
GENT AND FRIGHTENING MCS IN
ENTEEN, HE MADE AN INDELIB
BULLY ON THE LEADERS OF TH
FUTURE WITHOUT A PAST (199
STYLE WAS OFTEN DELIVERED I
TWO ALBUMS, BUSTA BROKE OU
EXPLOSIVE PERSONA WITH THE
SQUAD. HE CONSTRUCTED PRO
FUL PUNS EVERYWHERE AS IF
CLASSIC WRITING MANUAL, *THE*
BUSTA'S SOLO DEBUT DIDN'T C
GOLD) HE WAS ALREADY PERMAN
FILM COMMUNITIES WITH HIS
SINGLETON'S *HIGHER LEARNING*
HIP-HOP'S MOST MINDFULLY ME
CALLED QUEST'S "SCENARIO" A
"FLAVA IN YA EAR," ALSO STAR
COOL J. AND RAMPAGE THE
RELEASED *WHEN DISASTER STR*
SONG (AND SUPA-DUPA FLY VID
OUT OF THEIR MINDS, BODIES,
HANDS WHERE MY EYES CAN'S
BUSTA. NO ONE IN HIP-HOP IS
AND RAMBUNCTIOUS THAN BUS
STYLE IS UNFORGETTABLE AND

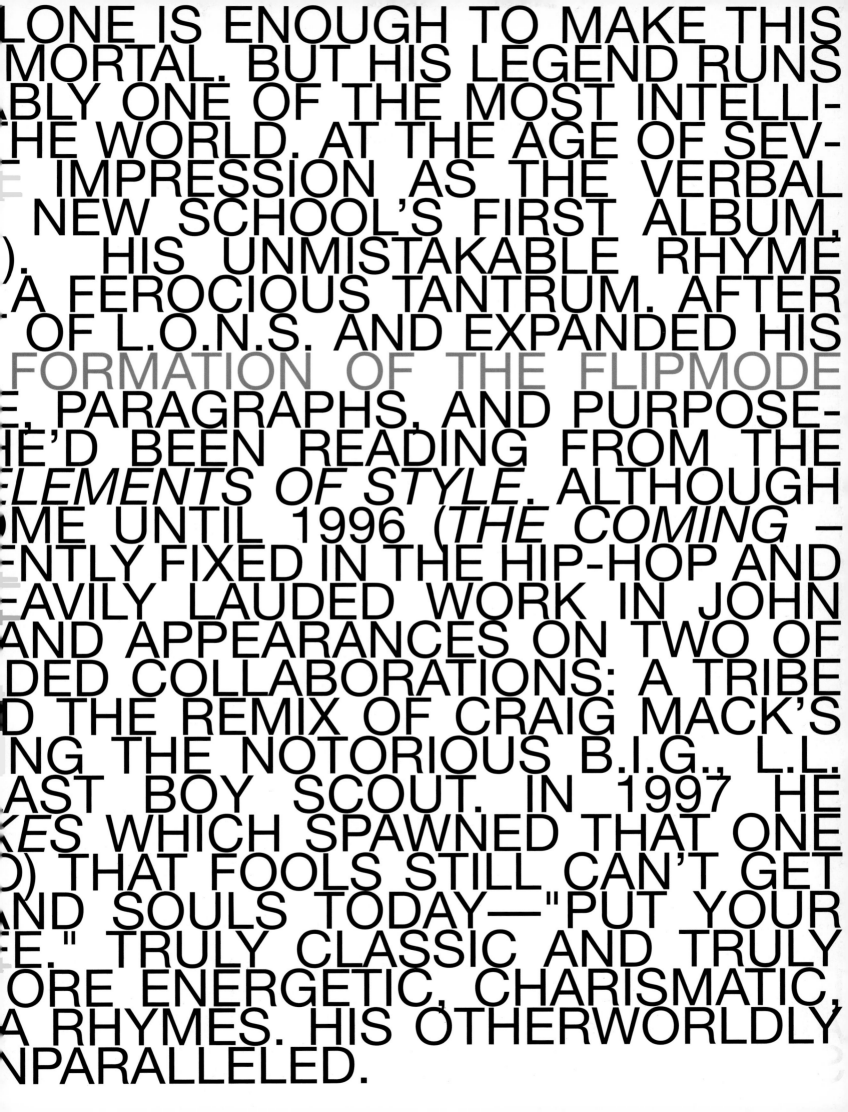

LONE IS ENOUGH TO MAKE THIS
MORTAL. BUT HIS LEGEND RUNS
BLY ONE OF THE MOST INTELLI-
HE WORLD. AT THE AGE OF SEV-
IMPRESSION AS THE VERBAL
NEW SCHOOL'S FIRST ALBUM.
). HIS UNMISTAKABLE RHYME
A FEROCIOUS TANTRUM. AFTER
OF L.O.N.S. AND EXPANDED HIS
FORMATION OF THE FLIPMODE
PARAGRAPHS, AND PURPOSE-
E'D BEEN READING FROM THE
LEMENTS OF STYLE. ALTHOUGH
ME UNTIL 1996 (THE COMING –
NTLY FIXED IN THE HIP-HOP AND
AVILY LAUDED WORK IN JOHN
AND APPEARANCES ON TWO OF
DED COLLABORATIONS: A TRIBE
D THE REMIX OF CRAIG MACK'S
NG THE NOTORIOUS B.I.G., L.L.
AST BOY SCOUT. IN 1997 HE
ES WHICH SPAWNED THAT ONE
) THAT FOOLS STILL CAN'T GET
ND SOULS TODAY—"PUT YOUR
E." TRULY CLASSIC AND TRULY
ORE ENERGETIC, CHARISMATIC,
A RHYMES. HIS OTHERWORLDLY
NPARALLELED.

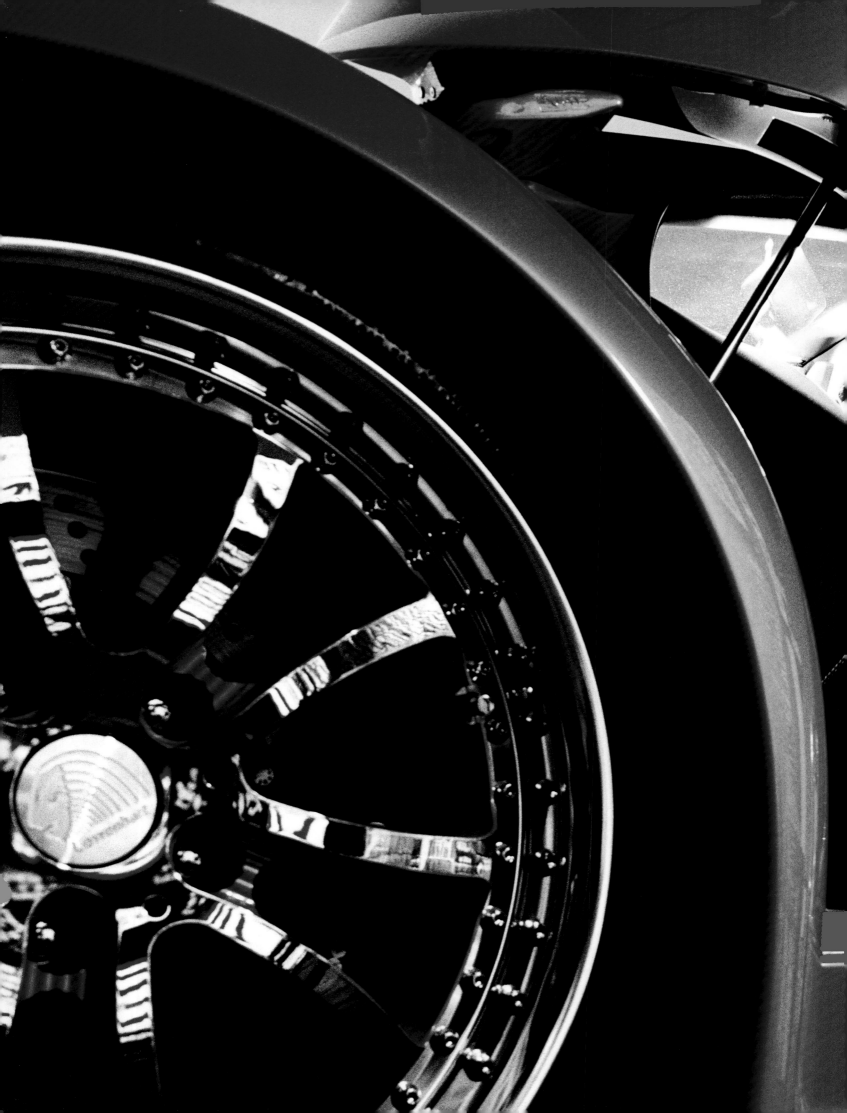

Kurtis Blow

During a Sugarhill party for Silvia

Kurtis Blow

During a Sugarhill party for Silvia Robinson held at the Audubon Theater in Spanish Harlem, Kurtis Blow and Russell Rush showed up with a new single. They were lookin' for their main man, DJ AJ, who was one of several DJs spinning that night. Rush handed the single with $500.00 in the sleeve to AJ, who could not be bought, and asked him to play it right away. Without disrespecting his man, AJ told him he couldn't just play his joint over someone else's set. After heavy naggin' he threw it on with headphones and started smiling. He faded in some of the song in between group set ups so no one could beef. They were diggin' it. AJ said, "Y'all wanna hear Kurtis Blow do his new song?!" The crowd was crazy. Kurtis Blow took the stage, skipping a line up of Grandmaster Flash, Wizard Theodore, and other T-Connection greats and performed for the first time, "Christmas Rappin'." That night immortalized Kurtis Blow in the midst of his contemporaries and launched Russell Simmons' career. Later, he thanked his friend for givin' him that break at the Audubon Ballroom with a dedication record. That record was AJ Scratch.

Fat Joe

A.K.A. CRACK I.S., ONE OF THE MOST FEARED GRAFFITI WRITERS IN TH
BRONX. I ADDRESS HIM AS MASSERIA, THE FORMER MOB BOSS OF THA
BOROUGH. WHY'S THAT? 'CAUSE IN THE MID EIGHTIES THROUGH THE PR
DOT COM ERA, TERROR SQUAD WAS BOMBING THE 6 LINE WITH NO OTHE
COMPETITION EXCEPT RISE AND THE 357 CREW. JOE STARTED HIS GHETT
WRITING CAREER AT THE AGE OF TWELVE AND THROUGH GRAFFITI HE WA
ABLE TO MEET CREWS FROM
ALL AGES, RACES & FACES. BY THE TIME VIDEO MUSIC BOX'S RALP
MCDANIEL'S SUGGESTED WE TALK, HE WAS ALREADY A STREET LEGEND
RUMOR HAS IT THAT CRACK ALSO HAD THE

STREETS BANGIN' AS WELL, WITH PERMANENT TAGS SPANNING FRO
THIRD AVE. TO CO-OP CITY. HIS FIRST APPEARANCE DOWNTOWN WAS A
S.O.B.S AT THE RAP-MEETS-POETRY SESSIONS CALLED, FLIPPING T
SCRIPT. INTRODUCING HIMSELF AS FAT JOE DA GANGSTER (THE FIRST M
IN TWENTY SEVEN YEARS TO CALL THEMSELVES BY THAT NAME AND TITL
CRACK STEPPED ON STAGE WITH A FAMILY SIZE BOTTLE OF SCOPE AN
TORE THE SCRIPT UP! IT WAS HIS WAY OF TELLING THE COMPETITION T
WATCH YOUR MOUTH WHEN YOU SPIT LYRICS, ALTHOUGH NO RHYMES WER
SAID TO THAT

EFFECT AND NO EXPLANATION WAS EVER GIVEN AS TO WHY THE MOUTH
WASH. HE HAS COMMANDED THE STAGE EVER SINCE. FAT JOE IS EXACTL
WHO HE SAYS HE IS (A GANGSTER). HE IS THE CAPO OF HIS OWN CREW AN
IS A BIG BROTHER AND FATHER FIGURE TO "MADE GUYS" UNDER HIS PRO
TECTION. IF I EVER HAD BEEF UPTOWN, I WOULDN'T HESITATE TO HAVE HI
SETTLE IT OUT OF COURT. THE TYPE OF MAN WHO'D REMEMBER MEETIN
YOU AT HIS FIRST PERFORMANCE AND WRITE YOU OFF FOR NOT ATTENDIN
PUN'S FUNERAL. HE GREW UP IN THE HEART OF THE HIP-HOP GARDEN O
DREAMIN', AND HAS EARNED THE RESPECT FROM THE ENTIRE INDUSTRY A
ONE WHO APPRECIATES EVERY ASPECT OF OUR UNIFYING CULTURE. PLUS
HE ONES THE LICENSE TO BRITISH WALKERS. WHAT?!!

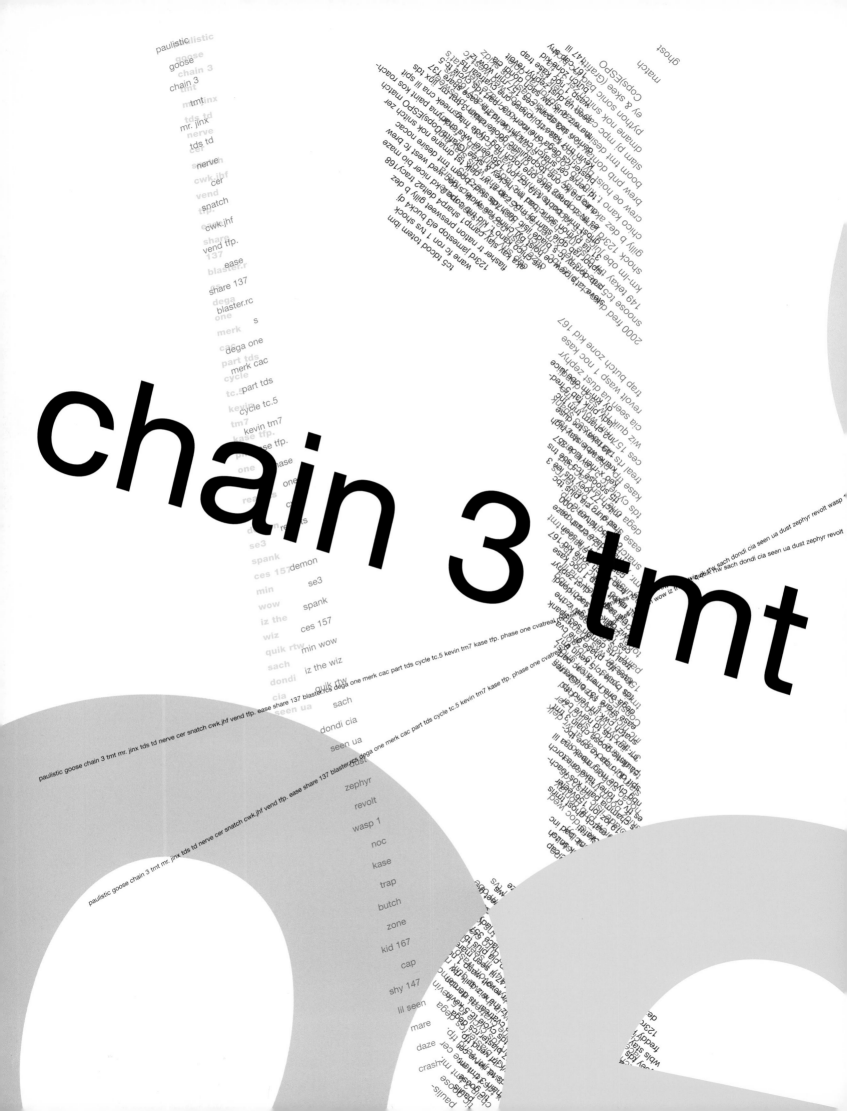

paulistic

goose

chain 3

tmt

mr. jinx

tds td

nerve

cer

snatch

cwk jhf

vend tfp.

ease

share 137

...butch zone kid 167 cap shy 147 lil seen mare daze crash paze cey roc futura 2000 fred duro cia plus tbc mitch 77 joey tds lee 3 tf5 snoose tc5 soe tns keo x-men lace 357 krane wbls stay high 149 tekay tnr duse in2 charm trim tnc lady pink fab 5 freddy km-lm obe juice tc5 tdcod totem ibm wane fc ron 1 tvs

paulistic
goose
chain 3
tmt
mr. jinx
tds td
nerve
cer
snatch
cwk jhf
vend tfp.
ease
share 137
blaster cs
cycle fred duro
think cac
pari tds
cycle tc.5
kevin tmz
paze tfp:
phase one
demon
se3 cvat
real rts
ces 157
min wow demon
iz the wiz se3
quik spank

sach   A-One, LES
CVAT-KP & AT, WR
dondi cia   DELK TST
LIL SEEN- SEEN TC. 5
seen ua   SNOOZE TC.5
KEL FIRST
dust   MAGOO TNR
spank   BG183
HOIST-BYI
zep ces   WANE-COD
ces   AD1
revolt 157   CS TAX, TFK
137   TRECH BYI
ATCO KOS
wasp 1 min   SABARA & SP1
min wow   WEBER TC.5
noc wow   EBN
iz the wiz   JAMES TOP
kase iz the   PRINCE AKAY KOS
quik rtw   DEZ TNT
CS, AD TAX
trap sach wiz   WOLF AOK
TEAM NTA
butch quik rtw   A.I. ONE
dondi cia sach   SKEME TNT
DONDI
zone seen ua   MED
VIC 20
kid 167 dondi cia   MR. DISCO
dust   EBN
cap seen ua   RICH RTW
zephyr   BOE WOW
shy 147 revolt dust   JOZ 156
JA ONE
lil seen wasp 1 zephyr   FUTURA
BRUO PNB
mare noc revolt   CESONE FX
DR. REVOLT
daze kase wasp 1   ZEPHYR
GHOST RIS
crash trap noc   DOZE TC.5
ESPO
paze butch kase   OAMP
KAZE FBA
cey roc zone trap   DUSTER
KAVES LOB
futura 2000 kid 167 butch   BABY 168, TVS

fred cap zone

Tagging

Kool Herc

"But the great man is he who in the midst of the crowd keeps with perfect sweetness the independence of solitude." These words were whispered one sunny day at the Rock Steady Anniversary as Kool Herc, the Father of Hip-Hop, flew an H-kite high above the packed park. To me, the kite was symbolic of hip-hop of how far and high it still can ascend from the ghetto streets. But it was painful to see someone that great and that revered, unapproachable to his children. This man you see in this picture created a social phenomenon that has grown so vast that the strongest leader couldn't contain it. In Sedgewick Projects in 1972 he charged 25 cents to hear breakbeats for six hours. Today, a top rapper makes $25 G'z a song per show. Maybe he thought we forgot him? Or because rap stars were flourishing that we didn't need him any more? Dead that! Bambaataa recognizes Herc as the architect who designed the prototype and so do we. Let's think of hip-hop, in this case, as a highly innovative company under the guidance of chief executive Kool Herc, who created an environment where ideas and innovations rise up from its lowest levels. The chief executive can prosper without the company, but if the company is a failure, then so is the chief. There are many chiefs still to come but there's only one legitimate

CHAIRMAN.

scarface

Scarface put Houston, Texas on the map. As a lifetime member of the Geto Boys, Mr. Untouchable reintroduced himself with his self-titled solo album in 1991. By 1994, he broke out of regional success with *The Diary*. The joint that did it for him? "Game Over!" Without question! If there is a reason to fear him, it isn't just for the things he does on his personal time. It's because of this rhyme: "Lord please murder my enemies/ Burn em' at a thousand degrees/ And Lord please let me make more cheese/ Cause I ain't quite ready to leave." Gimme a break. That's Dr. Dre, Too Short, and Ice Cube spitting that morning prayer with him. Rap-A-Lot Records soared to the top of the charts during those years, and why not, there was no competition! Scarface is the neighborhood bully's bully. He is a man who loves the black community—continually investing an unprecedented amount of money in Houston's school programs. Among other things, he's been called the pioneer of self-publishing. Rap-A-Lot, with the guidance of Mr. Untouchable, is a true syndicate.

Eric B. & Rakim

When we discussed the Kingdom and the Power in hip-hop I purposely left this part out to incorporate its explanation with Rakim's success. The Kingdom (Universal Zulu Nation) had the best DJs and MCs in the South Bronx and Harlem at the end of the seventies. But the Power came from the Five Percenters, taught by the ideologies of The Father Clarence 13 X Smith (formerly of the Nation of Islam). These MCs were blessed with lessons to study that dealt with complex mathematics and scientific equations. In the world of the superior lyricists, Rakim was/is the best. If there could ever be another teacher—or if The Father had chosen National Spokesman as The Honorable Elijah Muhammad did with Malcolm X—he would have chosen Rakim. Signed to 4th and Broadway Records under Cookie Gonzales, "The R" dropped the classic, *Paid in Full*. This was probably the first time a rapper showed money on an album. This symbolically sent out a message to all their fans and colleagues: *we gonna get this crunked out cheese and bake y'all 85s with knowledge, wisdom, and some shit y'all haters will never understand*. His first single "My Melody," was a musical assault of scratch patterns with a haunting whistle produced by partner in rhyme, Eric B. The B-Side was "Eric B. Is President," which introduced the concept of a DJ running the country and lobbying block parties to gain support. It worked. Those two songs were played everywhere that people gathered. His second album, *Follow The Leader*, had a stack of singles you could spin into heavy rotation. "Microphone Fiend," "Mahogany," "In The Ghetto," and the thug joint used in the feature film *Juice*, "Know The Ledge," all mark the career of a lyrical genius.

REMEMBER THE NIGHT KR
B'KLYN, NYC? IT WAS PAC
NEUTRALS ALIKE WATCH
WALK INTO A RECORD E
OPPORTUNITY TO GET A
OPENING VERSE OF HIS
WERE SHOT OUTSIDE TH
SHOW. THIS WAS 1985 AN
MOST, IT WAS A DIFFERE
MOMENT OF HIS LIFE N
REPORTER ONCE ASKED
GOING TO BE WHEN YOU
CALMLY, "I DON'T KNOW,
WHEN I'M THIRTY." COO
WON. STARTING WITH HI
RUSSELL SIMMONS AND
VERBAL EXCHANGE WITH
HOP IMMORTAL, KOOL M
THE CHAMPION WHO HA
THAN SIXTEEN YEARS A
MORE THAN ONE ALBUM
CAUGHT A LOT OF HIS
CESSFUL PEEKABOO STY
J AKA THE G.O.A.T. WIL
ITSELF AS AN INSULT TO

PS: WHAT HAPPENED TO

PINK

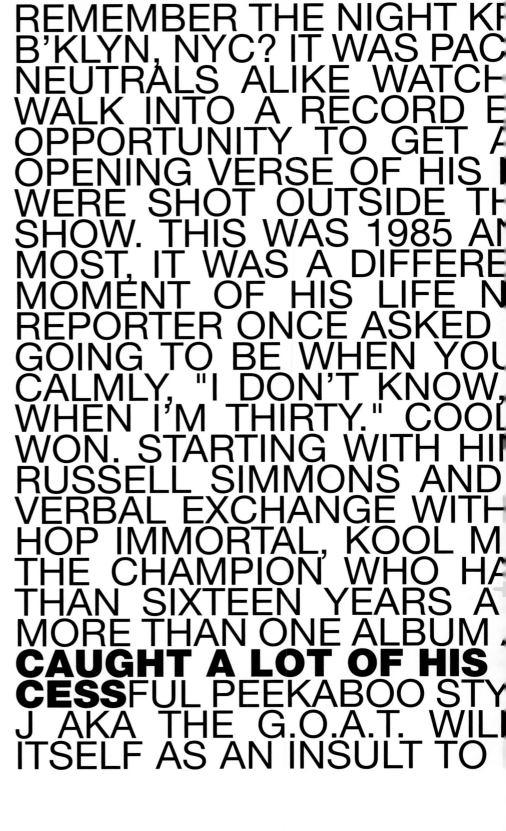

SH GROOVE HIT FULTON ST. IN DOWNTOWN
ED TO CAPACITY WITH GANG MEMBERS AND
G THIS KID WITH A LIGHT BLUE KANGOL
ECUTIVE'S OFFICE AND—IN A MOMENTARY
DEAL—SAY, "BOX" AND THEN RECITE THE
T SINGLE, "RADIO." ALTHOUGH THREE KIDS
THEATER AFTERWARDS, IT WAS A GREAT
THE BEGINNING OF THE CRACK ERA. FOR
T WORLD. FOR HIM IT WAS THE GREATEST
KT TO HAVING CHILDREN OF HIS OWN. A
M SNIDELY, "WHERE DO YOU THINK YOU'RE
RE THIRTY?" L.L., THE KING OF COOL, SAID
WHY DON'T YOU COME BACK AND SEE ME
WAS 19. HE'S BATTLED THE WORLD AND
SELF, THEN HIS LABEL MATE DJ RUN WHEN
ICK RUBIN RAN DEF JAM, THEN A SLIGHT
LA ROCK, THEN ON TO THE ALREADY HIP-
E DEE OF THE TREACHEROUS THREE. HE IS
PROVEN HIS STAYING POWER FOR MORE
THE TOP OF HIS NAME! L.L. WON'T DROP
YEAR BUT WHEN IT HITS, YOU KNOW IT. HE'S
PPONENTS OFF GUARD WITH THAT SUC-
E OF HIS. MR. SMITH AKA LADIES LOVE COOL
NEVER RETIRE. HE'D TAKE THE THOUGHT
MSELF, TO HIP-HOP, AND TO HIS FANS.

KEY D?

COOKIES

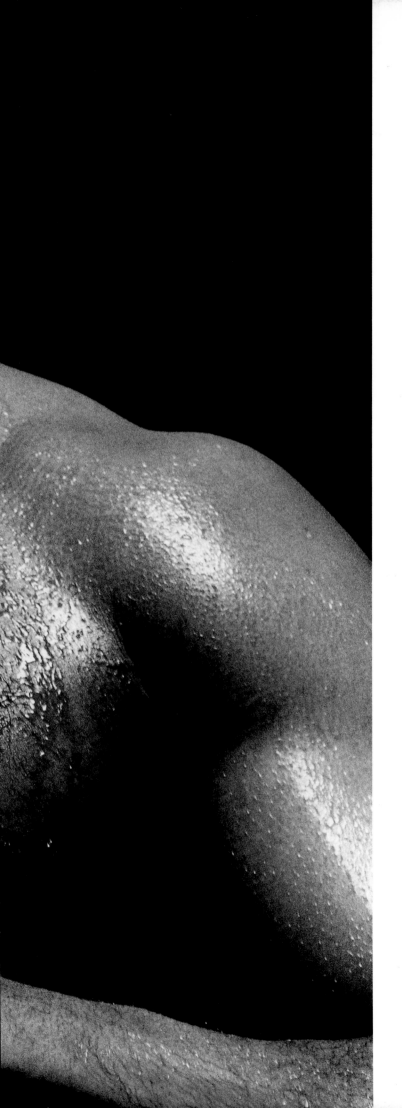

Missy Elliott

Don't let the name fool you, her joints are strictly felonious. Since 1996, she's been droppin' straight soap, cleanin' up the game, and stackin' chips like the lucky do. With Timbaland and Magoo—her production team and childhood homies—Missy platformed a rapid fire, stop... then blast forward, southernplayalistic style that made her records disappear off shelves faster than Tylenol bottles during the arsenic scare of the eighties. The title of her 1997 debut album, *Supa Dupa Fly* (1997), is an audacious understatement of its supreme flavor. Simplicity is the main ingredient in Missy's lyrics but her productions are anything but basic. If you didn't know any better you'd think you were having some sort of LSD hallucination after seeing the video for "Rain (Supa Dupa Fly)." Following in Busta Rhymes' footsteps, much of the video was shot through a fish-eye lens (before this style hit the big time) and Missy was donning wild get-ups in every shot; from the oversized patent leather garbage bag to the Jetson-style space suit. But making her own hit records was something Missy did in-between producing every other great artist's fly joints. The late nineties and new millennium saw Missy as the hit-single go to girl for everyone that was anyone in the music world: Whitney Houston, Aaliyah, Mariah Carey, Lil' Kim, and Method Man to name only a few. There was no missing with Missy. She followed up her debut with 1999's *Da Real World*—another platinum success which was most notable for the bounce-heavy single, "She's A Bitch." 2001's *Miss E "So Addictive"* featured an unlikely but celebrated collaboration with the versatile, Portuguese native, Nelly Furtado for the re-mix of "Get Ur Freak On," which is exactly what we did. Not one to be pigeonholed as only a supa dupa rhyme sayer, Missy flexed her vocal range on the 2001 female anthem "One Minute Man," giving all those bubble-gum poppers an effortless run for their money. In no time flat, Ms. Elliott bogarted her way into ghost writing, production, and artist management quickly transforming herself into a mogul of massive proportions.

Beastie Boys

There are certain artists in this book who may waver on the fence of immortality and then there are ones that are indisputable legends. King Ad Rock, MCA, and Mike D are of the latter category. This trailblazing trio began their markings as immortals by being the first all white rap group to dominate the hip-hop scene which, at the time, was ruled by black MCs. Credit Russell Simmons and Rick Rubin for signing the Beastie Boys to Def Jam in 1985 and recognizing one of the most novel hip-hop groups the world has ever seen. Their first single, "Fight for Your Right," introduced the unlikely, but ever popular, marriage of rock and hip-hop. With Volkswagen emblems, sunglasses, caps tilted to the side, and the exaggerated b-boy movements, it was impossible to take these New York City, Jewish kids seriously as rappers. But if they were good enough to open for label mates Run-D.M.C—who openly endorsed the Beastie's—then they were good enough for other heads who soon realized that "No Sleep Til Brooklyn" was the jam as was nearly every song off their first album. The enormous success of *License to Ill* brought on a hip-hop awakening to millions of rural and suburban teenagers who had minimal exposure to rap music. The 1989 release of their second album, *Paul's Boutique,* left critics and listeners alike stunned by its ingenuity. Again, they were responsible for the innovation of a new sound. This time their musical recipe melded punk, pop, and psychedelic together which was immediately embraced by both hip-hop and rock fans. They are justly credited as being the first—and best—to deliver the rock/rap milkshake and groups such as Korn and Limp Bizkit have the Beasties to thank for pioneering and perfecting a trend that ruled much of the airwaves in the late nineties and new millennium. In addition to one box-set and five US albums (1992's *Check Your Head* and 1994's *Ill Communication* are both excellent contributions to the artform, the Beasties parlayed their success into the vastly popular Tibetan Freedom Concert and numerous other political and social causes. Their superb artistry has always had something for everyone and as much as they veer to the punk and rock they always give something for the hip-hop purists.

A man of
honor and
impecca-
ble char-
acter. We

love him very much. He is as timeless as his stories and is immortal-ized with the high-est deco-rations a

Rap
General
can
receive.
'Maximum
respect,

brethren!
Fuh' tru,
YA
'ERE?!
'Forevuh'
Jah

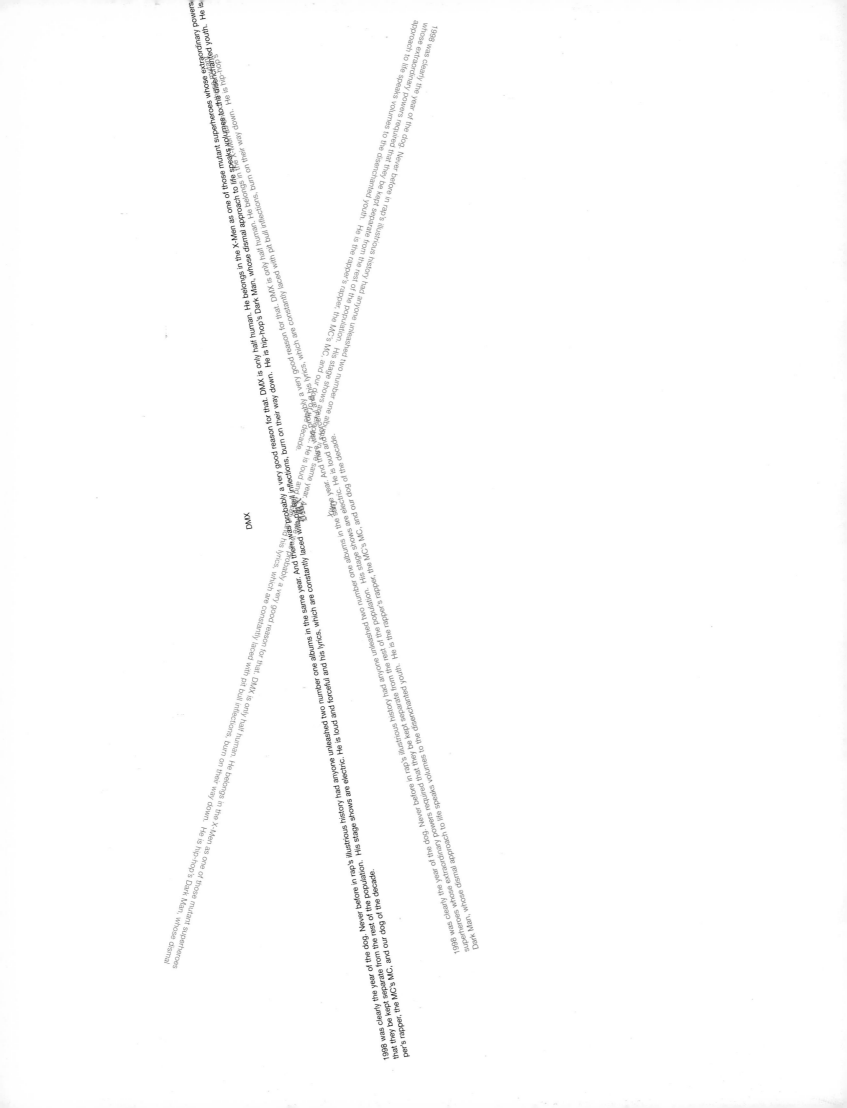

DMX

1998 was clearly the year of the dog. Never before in rap's illustrious history had anyone unleashed two number one albums in the same year. And there was probably a very good reason for that. DMX is only half human. He belongs in the X-Men as one of those mutant superheroes whose extraordinary powers required that they be kept separate from the rest of the population. His stage shows are electric. He is loud and forceful and his lyrics, which are constantly laced with pit bull inflections, burn on their way down. He is hip-hop's Dark Man, whose dismal approach to life speaks volumes to the disenchanted youth. He is the rapper's rapper, the MC's MC, and our dog of the decade.

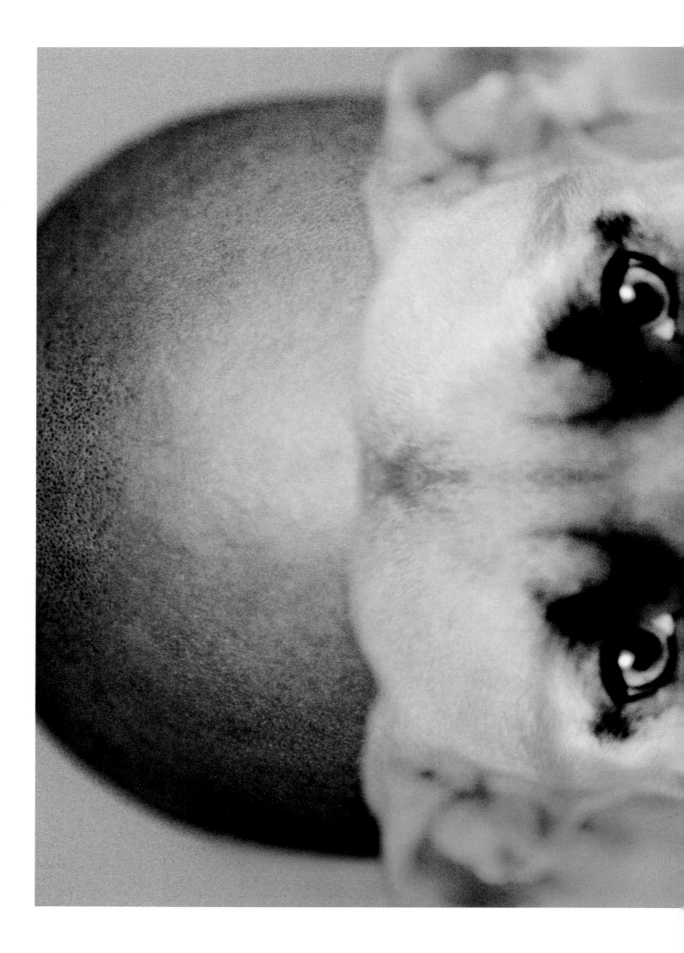

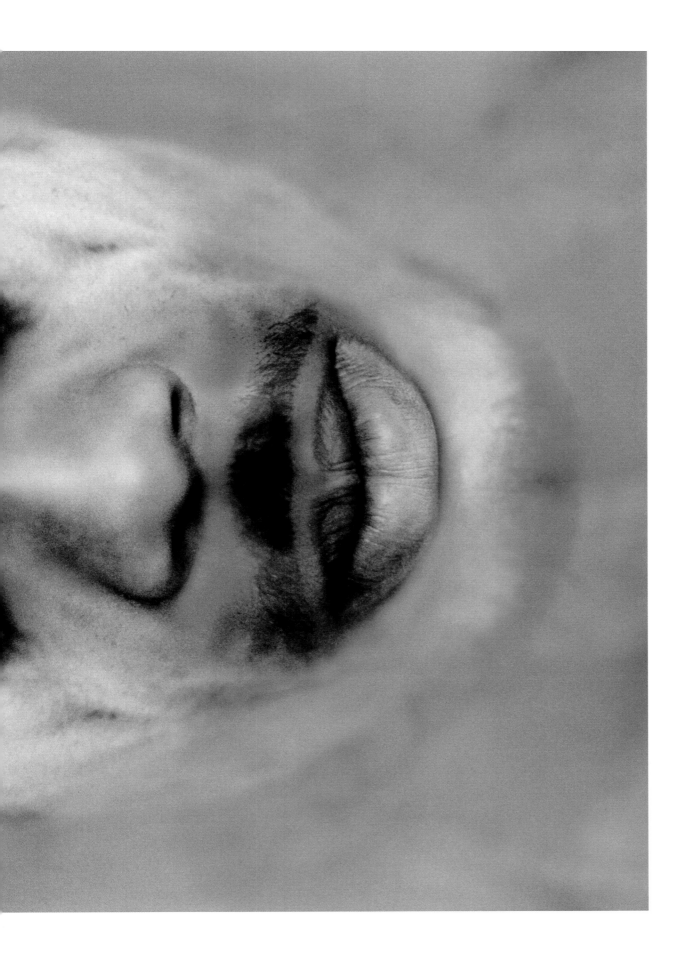

3rd Bass

If the myth that white men couldn't jump remained

true, then the myth that white men couldn't rap was

shattered when the world was introduced to MC

Serch and Prime Minister Pete Nice. They were

black—or so most people thought after hearing

their first single, "Steppin to the A.M." The video

revealed something astounding; there were some

new **White Boys** in town.

The black community ate them up too. Pete's sig-

nature cane carrying zoot suit style had the females

on pause. He was straight old school originality.

And MC Serch was awarded ghetto fame for spit-

tin' heat with the reigning impresarios of hip-hop

including Rakim, Big Daddy Kane, and Doug E.

Fresh. Because of his rigorous ongoing serching,

he remains one of the most educated and well read

MCs in hip-hop history. After two albums the

group disbanded but never disappeared. They

were Jackie Robinson-like trailblazers who demon-

strated true bravery and for that we salute them.

HOW MANY HIP-HO
SELL 14 MILLION
DEMO DEAL BRO
PIZZA SHOP? THE
ONE. AND IT COUL
THE TIMELESS S
DELIGHT" WAS T
THAT INSURED TH
BLACK MUSIC AR
MASTER GEE, WO
BIG HANK WERE T
AL INNOVATORS
WITHOUT COMPAR
THE MOST SIGNIF
TORS TO HIP-HOP

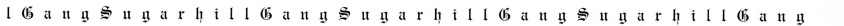

P ARTISTS COULD
RECORDS FROM A
ERED OUTSIDE A
ANSWER IS ONLY
BE ARGUED THAT
NGLE, "RAPPER'S
AT ONE SINGLE
FUTURE OF THIS
FORM FOREVER.
NDER MIKE, AND
HE ARCHITECTUR-
OF HIP-HOP.
ISON THEY WERE
CANT CONTRIBU-
N THEIR ERA.

MAN

Screw face rhymes he says.   He answers to many names.
Method Man
Screw face rhymes he says. Wu's prodigal son. He answers to many names.

Screw face rhymes he says. Wu's prodigal son. He answers to many names.

Screw face rhymes he says. Wu's prodigal son. He answers to many names.

Screw face rhymes he says. Wu's prodigal son. He answers to many names.

Screw face rhymes he says. Wu's prodigal son. He answers to many names.

Screw face rhymes he says. Wu's prodigal son. He answers to many names.

Screw face rhymes he says. Wu's prodigal son. He answers to many names.

Screw face rhymes he says. Wu's prodigal son. He answers to many names.

Wu's prodigal son.

The King Of New York
(Biggie Smalls)

May 21, 1972
to March 9, 1997

Biggie Smalls

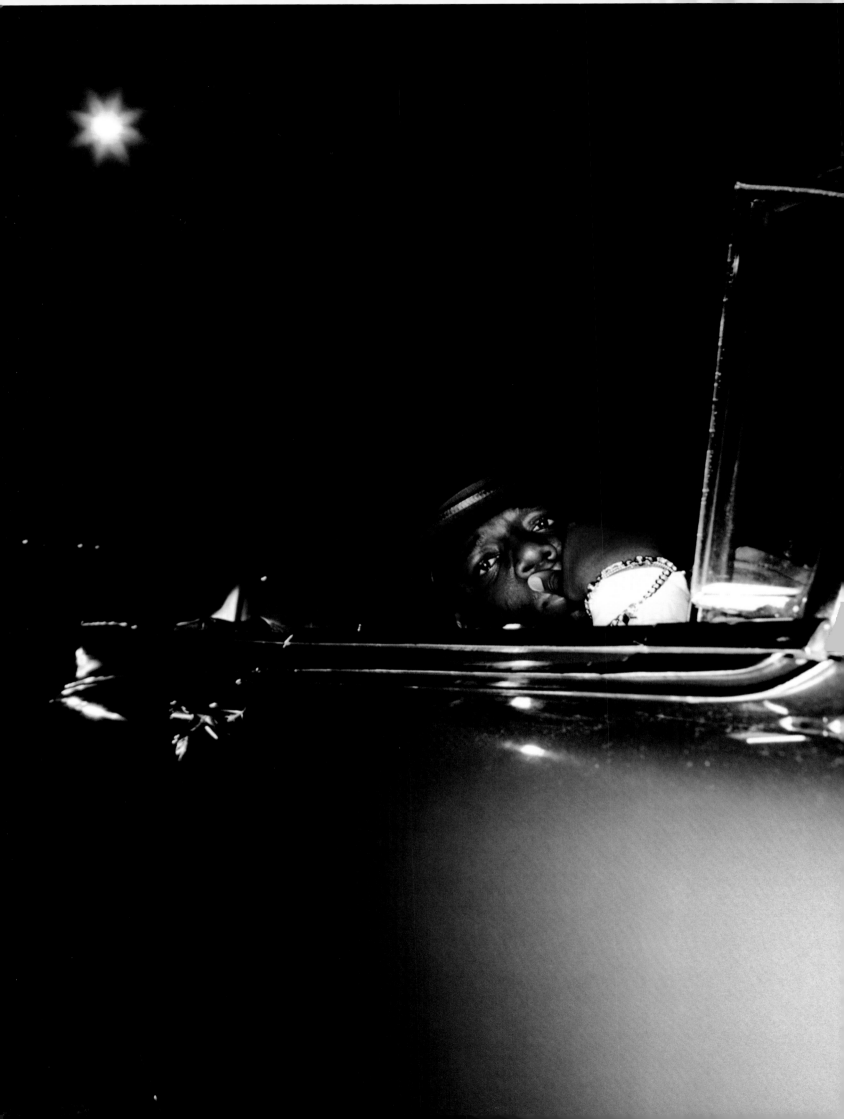

Rock Steady Crew

In California they called it Breakin' or Electric Boogaloo, but in New York, the foundation, they simply called it Rockin'. And steady rockin' is what the Rock Steady Crew is all about. Whether you were one of the originals to see them on 42nd Street when *WildStyle* was released or you recently caught them at a B-Boy Summit, these Ghetto Superheroes moved the crowd and themselves like nobody else. They elevated break dancing into an artform. Fusing martial arts, acrobatics, and body ego, the RSC made fans of nearly everyone that witnessed their mastery. Ask big Frank Sinatra or go rent *Flashdance* (they made an unforgettable ninety-second cameo) and you'll see why youth everywhere wanted to emulate these B-Boys. We watched them pull linoleum in the park, uprock and backspin with ski hats, goggles, and Pro Keds with Fat Laces. The legend continues today as the sons and daughters of these trailblazers keep on keeping on. Kuriaki, Buck 4(RIP), Ken Swift, Doze, Lady Doze, Baby Love, Pee Wee Dance, Frosty Freeze, Mr. Freeze, Jimmy D, Jojo, Alien Ness, Pop Master Fabel, Fever, Q-Unique, Swon, Tony Touch, Evil D, LiL legs, Mr. Wiggles and his sun Crazy Legs, and me: we salute you.

DDY KANE   SMOOTH OPERATOR.

BIG DADDY KANE   SMOOTH OPERATOR.

BIG DADDY KANE   SMOOTH OPERATOR.

BIG DADDY KANE   SMOOTH OPERATOR.

Big Daddy Kane   Smooth Operator.

LONG
LIVE
THE
KANE

Gang Starr

Gang Starr

Call them legends in the game. Whenever they advertise an album it gets got! DJ Premier is one of Brooklyn's finest beat misers. Guru, who was originally from Boston, is a man of distinction. *Daily Operation and Hard To Earn* are some of the best music done between 1992-1995. They've earned many stripes in this field but there is one accomplishment that distinguished itself from the rest of their accolades: jazz infusion Nobody was really checkin' for jazz when the fusion movement had just begun to grow up. That gave Gang Starr an edge. Using Elliot Horne's inspired poem, they came out with "Jazz Music." This contribution to the advancement of hip-hop can be equated to what Nirvana did for rock music with *Nevermind*. If you manage to find an unopened copy of *No More Mr. Nice Guy*, consider it a collector's item worth holding onto. It appears on Spike Lee's *Mo Better Blues*, with Brandford Marsalis, who would team up with Gang Starr for their follow up, *Step in the Arena*. Guru, the black Yul Bryner of rap, introduced music masterminds like Donald Byrd, Roy Ayers, and Ronnie Foste to a new generation. It was a much-welcomed time of enlightenment for hip-hop music. *Jazzmatazz* was their strongest tribute to these and other greats. The album is a living testament to their position as pioneers in this game.

Common

Chicago's South Paw B-Boy has the type of fame that only graffiti writers get. And although it took some time to put the south side of Chicago on the map, that is exactly what Common did. You have to *listen* to this lyricist to properly digest how complex his style is. If you blink, you'll miss something and most hip-hop fans missed his debut album, *Can I Borrow a Dollar,* because they didn't have the patience it required. But it is a gem and it attracted the best hip-hop had to offer. DJ Premier made room in his busy schedule to accommodate all the production on Common's sophomore album, *Resurection.* It seemed as though less sophisticated hip-hop fans had to be lead to this MC's lyrical fountain. Fans didn't find him on their own until he released the classic single "I Used to Love Her." Music enthusiasts everywhere quickly became familiar with one of the most creative artists in hip-hop.

Digital Underground

No one can front on D.U. They bombed the industry with ill voices, phrases, and multiple personas like their label mates, De La Soul did. Tommy Boy had another winner on deck with 2Pac, Chopmaster J, DJ Fuze, Shock-G, Jeremy "Jay-Z" Jackson, Money-B, and Schmoovy-Schmoov. They were by far, the best rap group to come out of Oakland. Of course they came with the traditional tribute to Parliament Funkadelic. That's like throwing a pitch to an old-timer on opening day. Gotta happen if your from the Yay. The magnificent seven were spearheaded by their captain of the clothes, Shock-G. His alter ego, Humpty-Hump (the ghetto Groucho Marx) made the name as famous as the sound itself. Their first and second albums were their moment. While every insider had a De La T-shirt, the Underground threw "Sex Packets" into the crowd when they took the stage. Inside had a latex condom, some jelly, a toy, and some kind of instruction booklet in Chinese. It was our chance to "Do The Humpty Hump" and in dem days, you didn't need to tell us twice. "Doowutchyalike," "Same Song," and "Kiss you Back" are all hip-hangin' anthems that brought out the Freaks of the industry. Digital Underground fit perfectly with The Daisy Age and their high energy shows were a blueprint for all hip-hop bands to follow for generations.

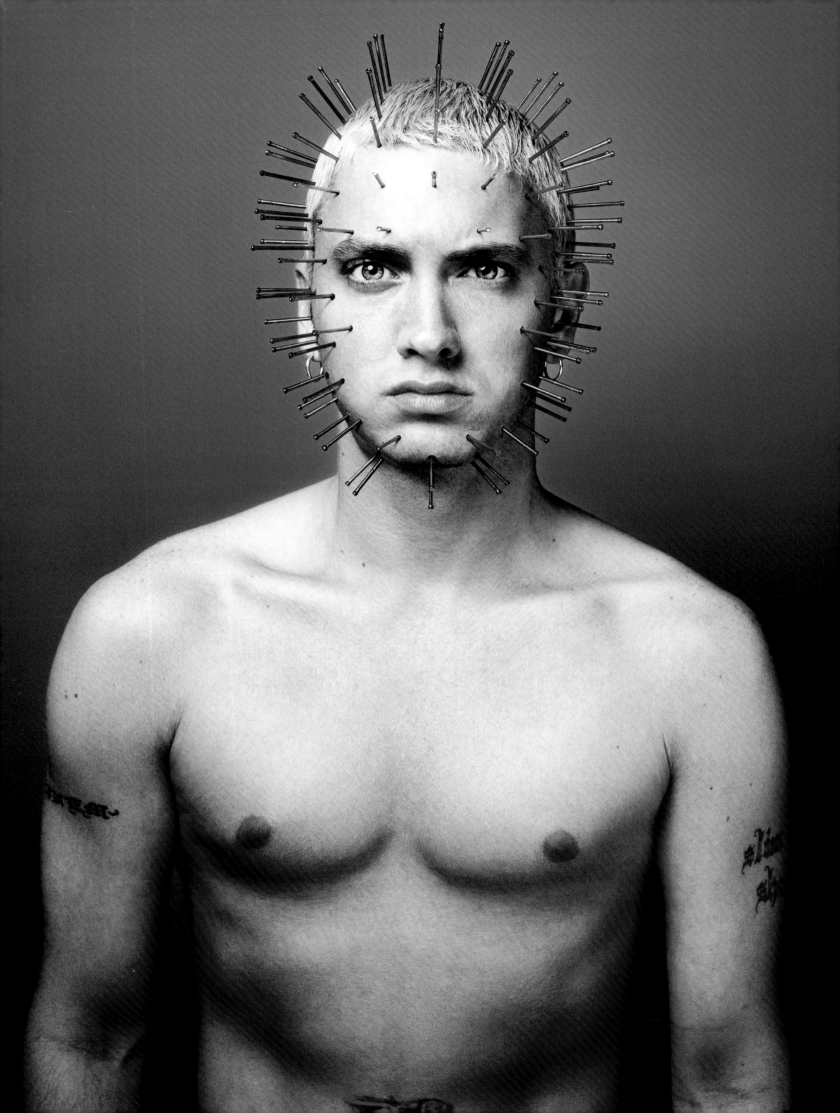

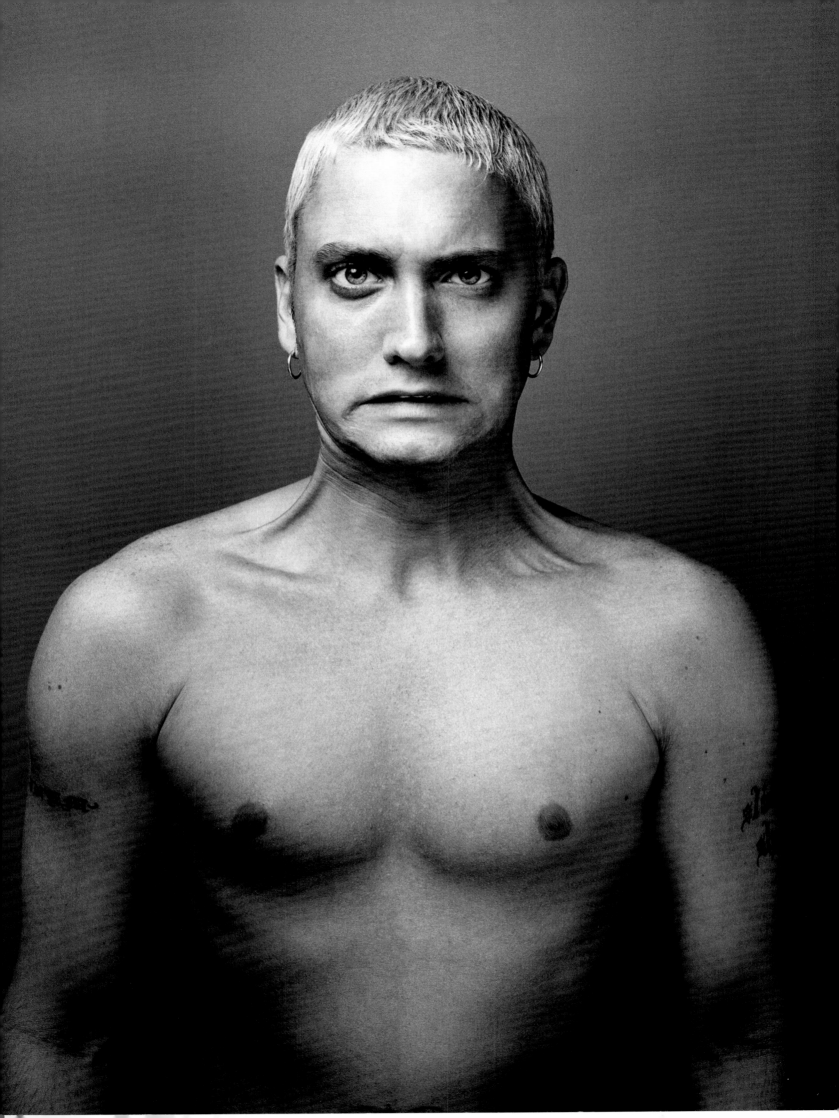

Xzibit

Xzibit

No one could argue
that X to the Z lead the
league in assists in
2001. He was the West
Coast go-to-guy for hit
single collabos and he
never disappointed.
Nate Dogg, Daz and
Kurupt, Eminem, Dre,
Snoop and the list
goes on. He has a
unique ability to shine
on someone's single
without stealing the
spotlight. We remem-
bered his raspy and
menacing voice from
the Likwit crew of
MCs from Northern
Cali, but began to
know him more inti-
mately while under the
auspices of legendary
producer Dr. Dre, who
produced Xzibit's third
solo album, *Restless*.
Some West Coast
extremists hailed him
as the new Snoop or
the new 2Pac but he
wasn't trying to be
either. He is however,
the torch carrying con-
tinuation of power-
house MC' s to hail
from the West Coast.

Outkast

For years it had been New York and Los Angeles. And then the Bay Area and Houston made their mark. And in the early nineties two high school buddies from Atlanta, GA got together to form a group that was previously known as 2 Shades Deep (aka Misfits Of The Outback) and slowly started a southern following that would reach a massive peak in 2000, branding ATL as the epicenter of the dirty South. Since their beginnings, Outkast members Antwan "Big Boi" Patton and Andre "Dre" Benjamin have never come wack on wax. They debuted with *Southernplayalisticadillacmuzik* (1994) and, although the celebrated singles "Players Ball" and "Funky Ride" barely crossed the Mason/Dixie line, that album was a major contribution to the artistic bettering of hip-hop. Outkast's second album, *ATLiens* (1996), was also tappin' and snappin' at mainstream turf but it wasn't until 1998 when Dre and Big Boi dropped their masterpiece *Aquemini* that heads on a global level started taking notice. *Aquemini* made a serious improvement to hip-hop's state of the union and received the highly coveted—and rarely given—five mics from *The Source* magazine. They say you're only as good as the last thing you put out and *Aquemini* was a near impossible album to top. But just two years later, in 2000, our ATLiens created their own planet on earth, *Stankonia*. The album went triple platinum within its first few months of release and was *the* album of 2000/01. Although "B.O.B." was the first bomb dropped, it was the long awaited apology to all the babies mamas' mamas that detonated a nuclear explosion. Their lyrics (delivered faster than a speeding bullet), their message (1/4 house party, 1/4 social commentary, 1/4 antagonistic but hardly misogynistic, 1/4 unintelligible), their style (1/2 ATL pimp, 1/2 uh… can't really say), their look (so fresh and so clean), and their personalities (1/2 on the Jimi Hendrix-veganed-out-tip man, 1/2 smooth-ass gangster) are far beyond comparison. Big Boi and Dre have taken hip-hop in a totally new direction and are two dirty South rap representatives that stank for colorful people and not just for people of color.

𝕺utkast

Nice & Smooth

For nearly eight years they were the kings of the 12 inch singles. There isn't a DJ—or shouldn't be one—who doesn't have Nice & Smooth's catalogue in their milk crates. Gregg Nice (Gregg Mays) and Smooth Bee (Daryl Barnes) put out four great albums containing no less than five legendary singles including: "Skill Trade," "We are Number One," "No Bones In Ice Cream," and "Sometimes I Rhyme Slow." 1994's Gang Starr collaboration—and permanent party staple—"Dwyck" is more than enough to immortalize Nice & Smooth. Although their music veered towards the hip-pop mainstream, they've always received crazy love and respect from the hip-hop community and their fans alike.

Nice & Smooth

For nearly eight years they were the kings of the 12 inch singles. There isn't a DJ—or shouldn't be one—who doesn't have Nice & Smooth's catalogue in their milk crates.

Nice & Smooth

For nearly eight years they were the kings of the 12 inch singles. There isn't a DJ—or shouldn't be one—who doesn't have Nice & Smooth's catalogue in their milk crates. Gregg Nice (Gregg Mays) and Smooth Bee (Daryl Barnes) put out four great albums containing no less than five legendary singles including: "Skill Trade," "We are Number One," "No Bones In Ice Cream," and "Sometimes I Rhyme Slow." 1994's Gang Starr collaboration—and permanent party staple—"Dwyck" is more than enough to immortalize Nice & Smooth. Although their music veered towards the hip-pop mainstream, they've always received crazy love and respect from the hip-hop community and their fans alike.

For nearly eight years they were the kings of the 12 inch singles. There isn't a DJ—or shouldn't be one—who doesn't have Nice & Smooth's catalogue in their milk crates. Gregg Nice

Gregg Nice (Gregg Mays) and Smooth Bee (Daryl

Some MCs are blessed by the
er lyrics that effortlessly wast
one of those chosen ones, Sir
Lana Moorer has been forcing
to shamefully bow down to
During the decade of the DJ
including the famous brawl be
champion, Lyte. Antoinette's
got the win for delivery. "Hot d
how she started the second ye
ical debut, *Lyte as a Rock* (198
force, and ask yourself, *If this*
ing, imagine the destruction th
case of full contact sport? You
because she showed us what
Eyes on This and 1993's *Ain*
"Ruffneck" garnered Lyte a 'Be
the first gold record for rap
female. There are a lot of MCs
and for good reason—but thei
Although heads revel in Lyte'
scene. Instead, she kept puttin
Bad as I Wanna Be), and a hi
Keepin' On"). She also kept it ri
rent crop of great MCs as she
virtually unheard but nonethe
(Pimp)" from his gem, *Like Wat*
checking the ego of her male
messages, MC Lyte has always
to, making her one of the grea

eavens with the voice to deliv-
their competition. MC Lyte is
she was old enough to talk,
nyone who wanted to battle her
heir commanding dominatrix.
many battles were recorded,
ween Antoinette and our sexy
nes were good; however Lyte
mn hoe here we go again..." is
se to "10% Dis" off her histor-
Listen to this record, hear her
only 10% of her tongue lash-
other 90% could employ in a
don't have to imagine, though,
else she had in her on 1989's
No Other. The classic single
t Rap Single' Grammy nod and
ngle ever achieved by a solo
om the past that disappeared—
music remained our nostalgia.
early work, she never left the
out a dope album here (1996's
single there (1996's "Keep On
e by collaborating with the cur-
d in 1999 with Common on his
ss great track "A Film Called
For Chocolate. Whether she's
ers or spreading anti-violence
said something worth listening
st orators of her time.

Mobb Deep

Prodigy and Havoc are the East Coast's answer to N.W.A. Their first video, "Hit It From The Back," portrayed a QB house party with naked girls on all fours giving up the oochie. For some strange reason the video never got past the reception area of the MTV offices. No one was ready for the Q.B. blitz led by these 15-year-old juvenile mobsters. Mobb Deep's unflinching characterizations of the Trife Life literally shook hip-hop's foundation. They left 4th and Broadway and signed with Loud Records in 1993. Soon after, they dropped *The Infamous*. It was murder on wax. They were flawless. "Shook Ones" was a steel pipe to the back of the head. It was a masterpiece single that let fans know, THERE ARE NO SUCH THINGS AS ACCI-DENTS. One year later they deaded it with *Hell On Earth*. Although critics pointed out that they were still rappin' about project hallways, crashin' expensive stolen cars, and piss drenched elevators that children got stuck up in, it didn't matter to hip-hop. While other half-ass rappers claimed hip-hop and it's alternative gang culture, Mobb Deep lived it. Thuggish beats and gully slanguage personified. *Murda Muzik* remains in demand without the crutch of commercial airplay. When they get down, it's always Double Trouble.

Naughty by Nature

Naughty by Nature

The early nineties were a boomin' time for hip-hop acts. What was once a grapevine oriented genre was now becoming a killer crossover industry and no group was as successful at going Top 40, while still evoking respect from the streets, as Naughty By Nature. In the late eighties, hype-man Vinnie Brown, producer Kay-Gee (Keir Gist), and front-man Treach (Anthony Kriss) were a broke and struggling rap group from East Orange, New Jersey when Queen Latifah took them under her wing. She signed them to her management company, Flavor Unit, and a deal ensued at her label, Tommy Boy. In 1991 they released their sensational self-titled album to rave reviews. Their first single, "O.P.P." was a tongue-twisted celebration of infidelity laid over a sample of the Jackson 5's "A.B.C." Overnight it became the ghetto anthem of 1992 and eventually the most famous acronym to come out of the hip-hop world. Treach's grimy style (black nylon vest, ski hat, boots, and padlocked chain around his neck) coupled with his thuggish good looks helped to establish him as a bona fide sex symbol which greatly contributed to the huge following NBN would accumulate. *19NaughtyIII* (1993) successfully evaded the sophomore jinx thanks largely to their second tongue-twisting phenomenon, "Hip-Hop Hooray." Ironically, it was their least popular album, *Poverty's Paradise*, which would finally garner them a much-deserved and long overdue Grammy for best rap album in 1995. Besides their musical offerings, NBN were also innovators of different facets of hip-hop style; they were one of the first rap groups to debut their own line of clothing (Naughty Gear) and they helped pioneer the hugely popular chillin'-in-the-projects-with-a-crowd-of-local-admirers video style that was an MTV staple in the mid to late nineties.

Mos Def

Among the most eclectic and heavily lauded MCs in hip-hop, Mos Def had been making important contributions to music long before his 1999 solo debut. At the age of nine he started his first group, Urban Thermo Dynamics, with his brother and sister. A new-school member of Afrika Bambaataa's famed Native Tongues, Mos Def was on the back burner on the De La Soul stove before he bubbled in the late nineties. In 1998 he and Talib Kweli made a successful attempt to reclaim hip-hop from its stupefying bling-bling mentality with the release of *Black Star*. Mos Def went solo in 1999 with the release of his diamond-in-the-ruff debut, *Black on Both Sides*. One of the most politically, socially, and musically important albums of the nineties, *Black on Both Sides* exists in a league all of its own. The first single, "Miss Fat Booty," was a great example of Mos Def's vibrant and intricate rhyme style but not a proper reflection of the depths of his trials. The punk-rock single "Rock & Roll"—a challenging dissection of the true roots of Rock and Roll—was a more accurate representation of his provocative nature and politically charged emotions. "Umi Says" was among a handful of songs which showcased Mos Def's instrumental talents (he plays bass, drums, and congas among other instruments) and captivating vocal ability. *Black on Both Sides* is one of the rarest of albums—in the same league as Biggie's *Ready to Die* and ATCQ's *Low End Theory*—that can be listened to beginning to end without fast-forwarding one second of one track. His impact on hip-hop continued with the 2001 release of the hit single "Oh No," also starring Pharoah Monche and Nate Dogg off of the *Lyricist Lounge Volume 2* album. But MC is only one of the titles beholden to Mos Def. His acting career (1994's "Cosby Mysteries," Spike Lee's *Bamboozled*) predates the rapper-turned-actor craze of the late nineties and his musical tendencies have lent themselves to the underground funk/rock sensation Black Jack Johnson. Everything about this Renaissance man embodies the re-birth of cool leaving no doubt that Mos Def most definitely is the Most Deffest.

Queen Latifah

The golden apple of The Flavor Unit, Queen Latifah began her hip-hop conquest in 1988 with the release of her first single, "Wrath of My Madness." A year later, the New Jersey native was signed to Tommy Boy records and released her landmark debut, *All Hail the Queen* (1989). After hearing "Ladies First" and "Dance For Me" it was difficult not to hail her. Latifah was not the first female MC in the game—she succeeded all-star pioneers MC Lyte and Roxanne Shante—but she is, without doubt, hip-hop's all-mighty matriarch. She is a born entertainer and her musical abilities have never been limited to strictly hip-hop. Instead, over the years she has flexed her reggae, R&B, soul, and lyrical prowess on wax. Witness the Queen's *Black Reign* (1993) as a delicious sampler of all the different flavors she served up. In 1991 Queen Latifah took notice of a struggling, up and coming New Jersey group, New Style. She took them under her wing and eventually they became labelmates of Latifah's at Tommy Boy. They released their self-titled debut album, *Naughty By Nature* and the rest, as they say, is history. Musical entertainment proved to be just one of her performance abilities. In 1993 she shifted gears when she took one of the leads on the hugely popular sitcom "Living Single," which ran for five years on Fox. All the while Ms. Owens was also popping up in feature films including: *Jungle Fever*, *House Party 2*, and most notably her indomitable breakthrough performance in *Set It Off* (which earned her an Independent Spirit Award nomination in 1997 for Best Supporting Female). In 1998 Latifah released her first album in five years (who had the time?) *Order In the Court* and if that wasn't enough she launched her own talk show, "The Queen Latifah Show," the following year. No other female in hip-hop could get away with the self-appointment of royalty except Latifah. Take one look at a childhood picture and it's evident that her mere presence dominated a room, undoubtedly demanding the title and throne she rightfully earned.

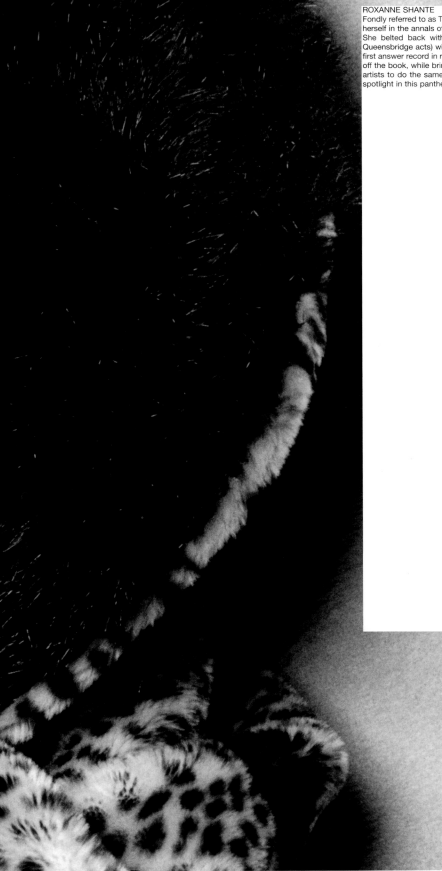

ROXANNE SHANTE

Fondly referred to as The Rose of Queensbridge, Roxanne Shante is a true legend. She created a place for herself in the annals of hip-hop by delivering an answer back to the U.T.F.O. classic, "Roxanne, Roxanne." She belted back with producers Fly Ty, Mister Magic, and Marley Marl **Roxanne Shanté** (the executive producer for Queensbridge acts) with "Roxanne's Revenge." She was years ahead of her time, deserving credit for the first answer record in rap history. She gave birth to the age of musical bat-

ROXANNE SHANTE

Fondly referred to as The Rose of Queensbridge, Roxanne Shante is a true legend. She created a place for herself in the annals of hip-hop by delivering an answer back to the U.T.F.O. classic, "Roxanne, Roxanne." She belted back with producers Fly Ty, Mister Magic, and Marley Marl (the executive producer for Queensbridge acts) with "Roxanne's Revenge." She was years ahead of her time, deserving credit for the first answer record in rap history. She gave birth to the age of musical battles. She's taxed rapper's on and off the book, while bringing back the birthright of the battle to include B. girls as MC's and inspiring many artists to do the same. Fortunately, her wars remained on wax. She earned our respect and deserves a spotlight in this pantheon of poetry.

Run-D.M.C.

4-ever the 1
for Jam Master Jay
by reg e gaines/ scratch
dj academy

from Hollis
the coolest
kindest
he ruled us
King from Queens
makin' hip hop pure pop
sportin' shells & cazals
rose to the top
breakin' beats
mixin' joints
straight from the streets
always on point
matchin'/patchin'/scratch
in'then hatchin'
shocked by the fame
he'd one day be catchin'
back in the day
made us all walk this way
now bands don't need
drums
or guitars to play
shined light on hard
times
never cried 'bout hard
knocks
decked in def/dope adi-
das
while rockin' the box
not 'bout gangs or no
guns
just parties and fun
Jam Master Jay
Forever the one…

Run-D.M.C.

For those who were stupid enough to think hip-hop was a passing phase, Run-D.M.C. put that notion to bed forever. It was impossible to prepare ourselves for what we know now as THE SECOND COMING OF COLD CRUSH! They rival the old guards of the skoolyard in a big way. Nobody heard of Queens when Flash and Caz were at a show. Crazy, if they were from that neighborhood, they couldn't fight and win. We have learned many truths since the beginning. One of them is that Queens has always had a hip-hop community growing underneath the foundation laid by The Bronx and Brooklyn's divine MCs. Run-D.M.C. became the Kings of Rap by way of influence (The Cold Crush Bros.). The in-between borough was unique in matching the DJing skills by former champions in the south and marrying them to lyrics inspired by knowledge of self taught by Islam and The 5% Nation. They put out the Greatest B-side record ever made, "Sucker MCs." A joint that no doubt made even Kool Herc smile. The High Guards now believe it outsold its commercial right-wing flip, "It's Like That," in the same commercial market. That's Hully Gully! They made the 2nd most legendary dress code trend in hip-hop history and haven't changed a thing. Everything about Darryl, Joe, and Jay is immortal. Their reluctant marriage to rock beats on their *King Of Rock* album was a masterstroke! There may never be a system that will be able to count that album's sales accurately. At the Def Summer Jam of that year, DJ Run ran shit with his gold chain, D.M.C had the O.E., and Jam Master Jay had a microphone on his mixer. It was like three Casanova Flies on stage at once. They are THE ONES who loved it even more than their Bronx neighbors. They were the first rap group on Dick Clark's American Bandstand. The first to have a sneaker endorsement, and the only group I've ever seen who still could make every living thing in Madison Square Garden on two legs take off their Adidas. (All Day I Dream About Sneakers) It wasn't easy for seventeen-year-olds to deal with touring and shows. They indulged in their success but make no mistake, these guys give all they've got and deserve credit for maintaining the best live show on earth. They made rap a force that could not be withstood. They legitimized disenfranchised youth. None would ever make fun of us again! Imagine if you were a multi-millionaire before your 19th birthday. How would you act and sound? Take a good look.

2Pac

June 16, 1971 –
September 13, 1996

He was the liveliest rapper in existence; a glowing attribute that also happened to be his tragic downfall. Tupac Shakur was a rose, thorns and all, that grew through concrete. He was too live for a crew and too tough to know when to let shit slide. Pac walked in, guns blazin', ready to be the best at any cost. In the movie *A Bronx Tale*, a question is asked by a child to a don: "Is it better to be loved or feared?" 2Pac was both. He loved the limelight but hated the eternal conflict that comes with street immortality. America was built by cowboys and gangsters and America Inc. loves a tough guy. So do women. Tupac Amaru Shakur was the most charismatic rapper/actor that ever touched both. Destined to step out of the background of Digital Underground, he made his move with his double platinum, solo debut, *2pacalypse Now*. He followed that up with his highly lauded film debut in *Juice*. *Strictly 4 My N.I.G.G.A.Z.* made him a main stay. One of his more laid back cuts, "I Get Around," is still the party favorite in our society. In 1993 2Pac appeared in the basketball drama *Above the Rim*, another role that portrayed him as an ox carrying gunman. He has the longest resume of any hip-hop artist. He gives new meaning to a catalogue and what it stands for. He excelled as an artist, producer, lyricist, and martyr. His legendary contributions—both platinum and criminal—started with his first album and have yet to cease adding up. He anchored Thug Life into our community. Taking aim at society and hitting the hearts and the charts of world youth; he further validated an ideology that lends to freedom with wealth. Those who were entrusted to look out for him failed us. With that kind of Midas touch power, he needed someone close to him to punch him in the face and say, "Who are you mad at!! Your enemy isn't as tough as you think. Neither are you!" Even in death he releases songs from the grave like a ghost who haunts without rest. Such power for one man to have! Not only his music, but also his presence, is felt in the present day. Now he's what he's always wanted to be—untouchable. No longer will he secretly fear harm befalling him. Never again shall he suffer the ills of those who don't love him. In time he may even forgive himself. We'll know soon enough. It will be recorded for us who serve as witnesses. He was our Lancelot. A knight of the crowned Death Row label. Alas, even immortals ain't perfect.

House of Pain

Notre Dame never had anything on these fellas. House of Pain showed us what it truly meant to be a shit-kickin', Mickey's guzzlin', proud Irishman. In the early nineties, high-school buddies Everlast (Erik Schrody) and Danny Boy (Daniel O'Connor) joined forces with DJ Lethal (who is inconsequently Latvian not Irish) and, under the production of Cypress Hill's DJ Muggs, released their self-titled debut album in 1992. You know what happened next. The song happened next. Some cats are in this book because of the massive impact their career—however long or short—had on the future course of hip-hop. Others are here because of their ability to produce one classic joint after another. But House of Pain has turned up on these pages mainly for creating the song that is synonymous with the summer of 1992 and with nearly every party anyone attended for the duration of the nineties: "Jump Around." Every person living in the United States and born on or after the year 1970 knows this song and if they don't it's because they were living in a shack in Montana. It was more infectious than the West Nile Virus. Years after its release it still shows up in movies, at parties, on commercials, and on the radio. We could end it at that but it wouldn't do HOP justice. *House Of Pain* (on which the song appeared) happens to be a justly classic album that was overshadowed by *the song*. "Danny Boy," "Top O' the Morning To You," "Put on Your Shit Kickers," and "Shamrocks and Shenanigans" were catchy parodies of Irish life and they made us all want to throw bottles of Irish Whiskey across the bar and start riots on St. Patrick's Day. Their second album, *Same as it Ever Was*, was released to rave reviews in 1994 and debuted at number 12 on the charts. However, the group was cursed by the enormous success of "Jump Around" and the album, although producing great joints such as "Who's The Man?," didn't carry our boys and neither did the hugely ignored *Truth Crushed to Earth Shall Rise Again*. But these men are tenacious. When the band broke up, DJ Lethal took an oh-so-small gig as Limp Bizkit's DJ and Everlast released his bluesy-rock solo album, *Whitey Ford Sings the Blues*, which went platinum proving that he may just last forever. And Danny Boy got a job… wait… where the hell are you Danny Boy?

IS SYNONYMOUS WIT
1992 AND WITH NEAR
ONE ATTENDED FOR
MAE IT'S
AROUN
PERSON LIVING IN TH
BORN ON OR AFT

H THE SUMMER OF
Y EVERY PARTY ANY-

BUMP

P.

EVERY

UNITED STATES AND

R THE YEAR 1970

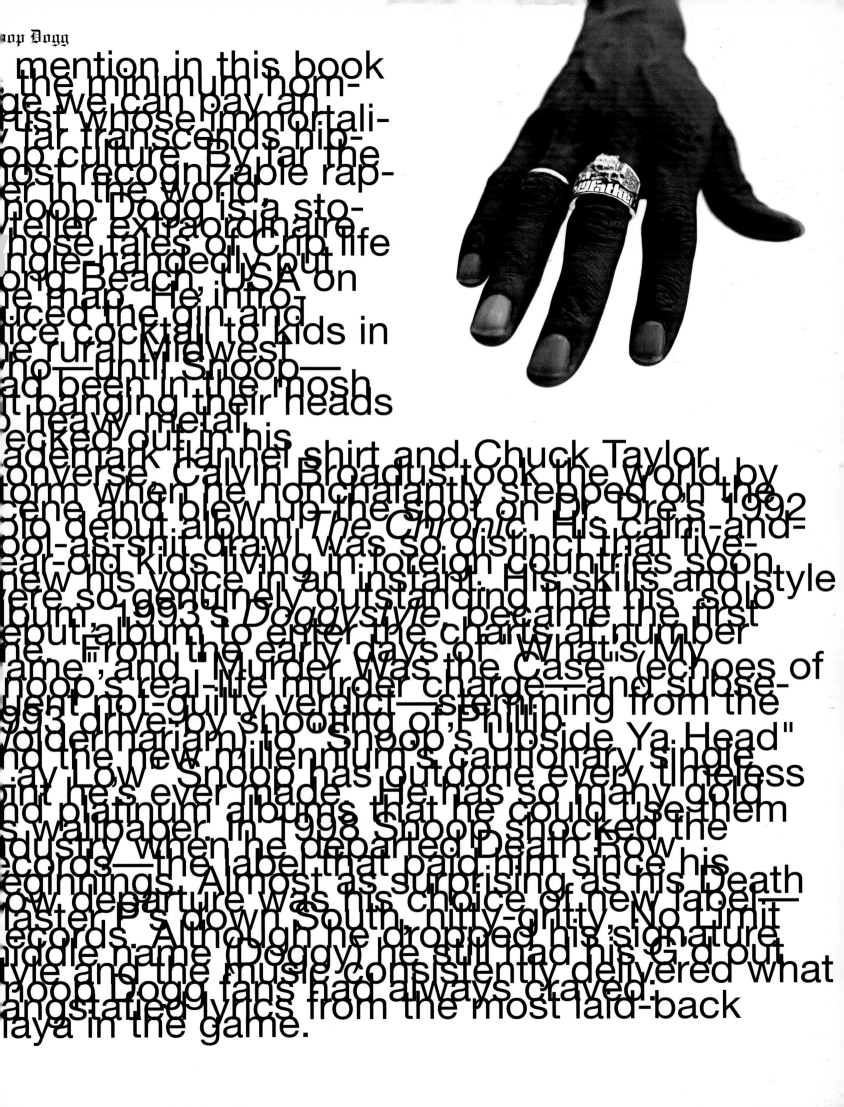

mention in this book
the minimum hom-
age we can pay an
artist whose immortali-
ty far transcends hip-
hop culture. By far the
most recognizable rap-
per in the world,
Snoop Dogg is a sto-
ryteller extraordinaire,
whose tales of Crip life
in Long Beach, USA on
the map. He intro-
duced the gin and
juice cocktail to kids in
the rural Midwest
who—until Snoop—
had been in the mosh
pit banging their heads
to heavy metal,
decked out in his
trademark flannel shirt and Chuck Taylor
Converse. Calvin Broadus took the world by
storm when he nonchalantly stepped on the
solo debut album *The Chronic*. His calm-and-
cool-as-shit drawl was so distinct that five-
year-old kids living in foreign countries soon
knew his voice in an instant. His skills and style
were so genuinely outstanding that his solo
debut album, 1993's *Doggystyle*, became the first
debut album to enter the charts at number
one. From the early days of "What's My
Name," and "Murder Was the Case" (echoes of
Snoop's real-life murder charge—and subsequent not-guilty verdict—stemming from the
1993 drive-by shooting of Philip
Woldermariam) to "Snoop's Upside Ya Head"
to the new millennium's cautionary single
"Lay Low," Snoop has outdone every timeless
joint he's ever made. He has so many gold
and platinum albums that he could use them
as wallpaper. In 1998 Snoop shocked the
industry when he departed Death Row
Records—the label that paid him since his
beginnings. Almost as surprising as his Death
Row departure was his choice of new label—
Master P's down-south, nitty-gritty No Limit
Records. Although he dropped his signature
middle name (Doggy) he still had his grip out
style and the music consistently delivered what
Snoop Dogg fans had always craved.
gangsta lyrics from the most laid-back
playa in the game.

Ludacris

In the late nineties, hip-hop's civil war was being fought and won by the South. A conquering army comprised of No Limit Soldiers, Cash Money Millionaires, Outkast, and Goodie Mob lead hip-hop culture in a southern direction. The survival of the dirty South had been secured, but complacency isn't a part of southern mentality. Enter Ludacris. Credit Scarface and Def Jam South for building the bandwagon that everybody seemed to jump on after Ludacris hit us with his first single, "What's Your Fantasy." What followed was a blitzkrieg of hit singles laced with some of the year's most unforgettable hooks. Without question, Ludacris was the rookie of the year in 2000. And like most rookie's of the year, he has the talent to one day wear a championship ring. DJ Lindy presiding!

"The South will rise again..."

The anatomy of the hip-hop bands

I bet you never thought you'd see the two greatest hip-
h   o   p

bands come together in one place. It took *Hip-Hop Immortals Vol. 1* to make it happen. And it's the only place you're gonna find them blowin' smoke like kisses to y'all. Peep it long and hard! These Brooklyn, Phillie blunt smokin' radicals spark jam sessions anywhere there's   a   lamppost.   Stetsasonic

was the original hip-hop band to rock the stage. They invented one of the greatest classics ever made, "Go Stetsa I!" The sound could be heard forever so when you see them in some Midwest mall, buying pampers and warm cereal, you can congratulate them for all of us who were there. For those who weren't, the torch was passed to   The

Roots, who remain the most dedicated group of hip-hop m   u   s   i   -

cians on the road of rap. They tour an unprecedented 335 days out of a year, blasting hits with an all-star Syndicate: Common,

Erykah Badu, Jill Scott, Jazzyfatnastees and The Okayplayer Organization. The Roots got OK Playaz from the old school as well. Scratch and Rahzell held down the turntables without needles! Like Rev. Martin Luther The King Jr., we have a dream too, and it's to hear these two groups rock together just once! That would be the real rapper's delight. No matter how nice a DJ could be, there's nothing that takes hip-hop to the next level like live instruments.

He's known as The Captain. The initials stand for professionalism, quality, experience, and durability. If there was ever an MC who could get a Government Contract for superior mic control, it would have to go to Grandmaster Cazmere! Now, y'all might not remember this but The Fantastic 5 and The Cold Crush Bros. started out around the same time. BET and MTV started at the same time too. Get the ball point? Caz is an example to all MCs in the critical era of discipline. It's the flip side to talent that usually decides who goes head first into the Hip-Hop Hall of Fame. Discipline is what former graffiti writers like us learn with hours of practice. It's also handy when your writing hot shit for other crews you've either battled or will. Thinkin' that some sucker MC was gonna bite his number 1 style, he brought latin DJ

Grandmaster Caz

Charlie Chase and his lyrical revolvers to his crib and tightened up their game for over a year and a half before they actually crushed competition. When their time came, the showmanship displayed by the Bros. made everyone else's styles prehistoric. They had the best choreographed show in the world of rap until Run-D.M.C came along. Caz's example of what a real DJ/rapper is supposed to be credits him as one of the first to deejay and MC simultaneously. The fresh, fly, wild, and bold Cazanova even had the balls to battle Bambaataa. He not only influenced rap's first superstars, DJ Run (an MC) and D.M.C. (the second coming of Caz), but also Funkmaster Flex, DJ Clue, and every mixtape DJ who pops dat cris while spinnin'!

Ecstasy, Jalil, and Grandmaster Dee were old school by the time Run-D.M.C. was getting non-stop airplay. Nobody except Bambaataa ever thought that mixing R&B with hip-hop would

become the norm form of today's music, but Whodini

Whodini

deserves mention for making this prediction. He was a daring artist who ventured into musical neighborhoods that were considered off limits to hip-hop. They were freaks but they were original freaks with perfectly manicured hair and nails with stretched leather blazers and matching rain hats. They're from Brooklyn's fanatical Wycoff Housing Projects but it was hard to see that in

those pretty faces.

They made a memo-

rable impact when

they dropped "Freaks Come Out At Night"

and "Friends." We celebrate them as being an integral part of hip-hop's adolescence.

Wu-Tang Clan

Know why Ghostface called his lead single, "Apollo Kids?" Because you can't boo them off the stage! There's no comp. That's how we back our boyz with the swords and hoods. Unconditionally. They represent more than Stapleton Housing project or Park Hill. The W is the remnant of 5% MCs that were the guardians of the books of life. Students of the 1-20, masters of the 360 degree ciphers held in front of the building. 1993 was the jump off for DEEP SPACE NINE. RZA played me "Protect Your Neck" and I fell out laughing. The flip side, Method Man, made me wet my pants! He explained this whole ancient sword style used by kung fu masters in the hills of China. It was over my head. When it dropped, the buzz swarmed the streets throughout the country. Hit men from every label offered them a deal. GZA, who I knew loved chess, was part of the hooded clansmen that waltzed around a checkerboard floor, ryhmin' in the low budget video. They had weapons and were poppin' that Ole Brooklyn lager the way only the Gods could. They elbowed their way in, started getting independent deals and separate royalty checks, bangin' the bosses like they were giving out free cheese! *Enter the Wu-Tang: 36 Chambers* was a juggernaut. The music industry got moved on like a chessboard and became a candy store hangout for the Clanbinos. With Meth a superstar and Grammy winner, Ol' Dirt McGirt getting lime, and GZA wackin' out labels, they expanded their operations into multiple industries: Personnel, Real Estate, Garment Industry, and Film. Their invincible congregation (made up of RZA Chief Abbot, GZA Maxi Million, Ol Dirty Bastard-Unique Ason, Johnny Blaze-the MZA, Shallah Raekwon-Lou Diamonds, Ghostface Killa-Ironman Starks, U-God 4-bar Killer-Golden Arms, Inspecta Deck-Rollie Fingers, and Masta Killa-Noodles) symbolizes the triumphant return of the Crew (The largest rap crew ever assembled. They don't need a theme and they don't need 16 bars apiece. Wu-Tang defines the profession called Mic Control. Every line is a freestyle session making you look out for Mr. Softee. Every day is like a video shoot enriched with books of life, bags of dro, hammers, 20 inch phat wips, wally slipperz, beehive fades, diamond ear studs, thick chains, pinky rings(on the southside only), 40 pairs of sneakers each(at least), all totaling around $64,000.00 vested in the fly shit, which could easily come undone at the smooth hands of beautiful women of any ethnicity or no pigmentation. There's no mistaking these supermodels who also MC. These are the type of brothers I was trained by. The ones who taught me style and what being a legend costs. Amongst all the families that exist, Wu-Tang are the Corleones of rap. A confederacy tree with offshoot branches: Killer Bees, Killer Army, Suns of Man, Brooklyn Zoo, P.L.O.s, and of course, every hip-hopper from the most slept on borough, Staten Island. If you don't protect your neck by keeping your head low one of these branches might cut off. Their business strategies of redefining wealth and its distribution aren't from the Wharton School. It comes from runnin' a House Gang up north while keepin' your commissary as crisp as your orange jumper. They embody Brooklyn hip-hop and are the finest at it no matter where they live!

Signed, Tom Hagen.

Wu-Tang Clan

Crash

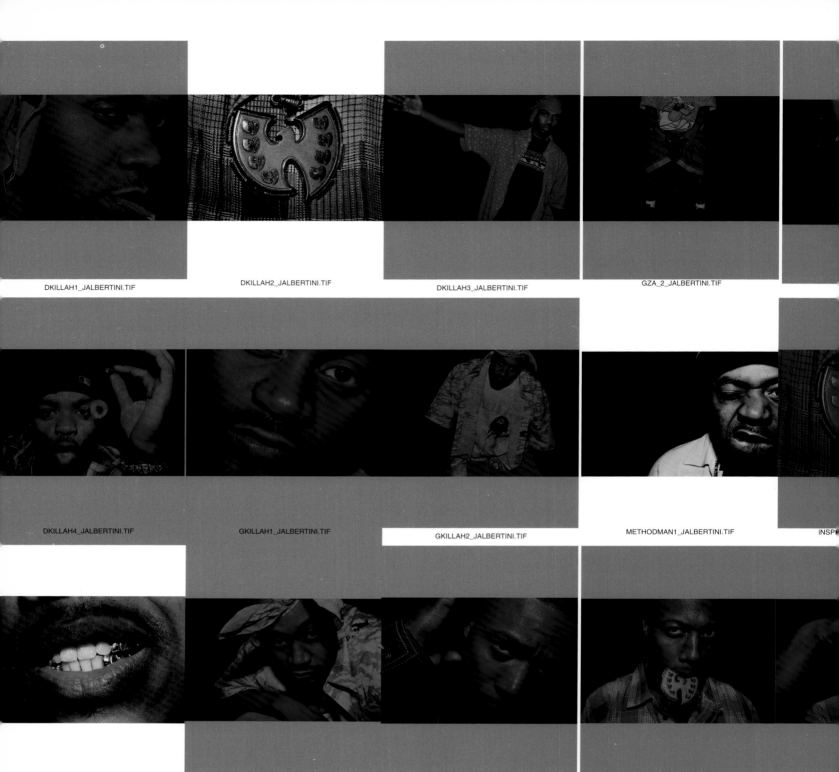

DKILLAH1_JALBERTINI.TIF   DKILLAH2_JALBERTINI.TIF   DKILLAH3_JALBERTINI.TIF   GZA_2_JALBERTINI.TIF

DKILLAH4_JALBERTINI.TIF   GKILLAH1_JALBERTINI.TIF   GKILLAH2_JALBERTINI.TIF   METHODMAN1_JALBERTINI.TIF   INSP

GKILLAH3_JALBERTINI.TIF   GKILLAH4_JALBERTINI.TIF   GZA_1_JALBERTINI.TIF   INSPECTADECK3_JALBERTINI.TIF   INSPE

RAEKWON5_JALBERTINI.TIF   U_GOD_3_JALBERTINI.TIF   U_GOD_4_JALBERTINI.TIF   U_GOD_5_JALBERTINI.TIF   R.

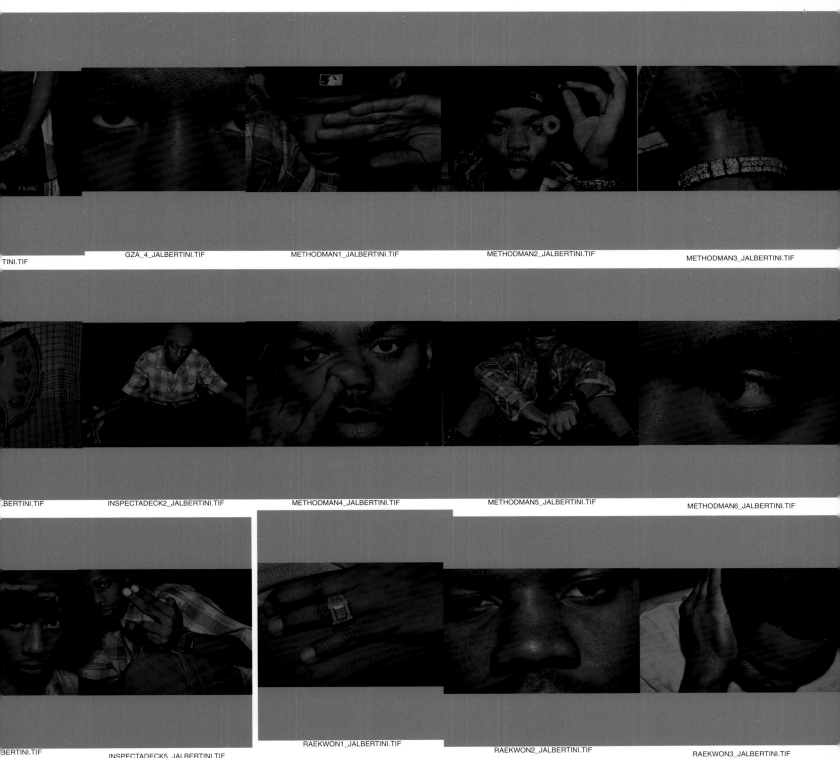

TINI.TIF   GZA_4_JALBERTINI.TIF   METHODMAN1_JALBERTINI.TIF   METHODMAN2_JALBERTINI.TIF   METHODMAN3_JALBERTINI.TIF

BERTINI.TIF   INSPECTADECK2_JALBERTINI.TIF   METHODMAN4_JALBERTINI.TIF   METHODMAN5_JALBERTINI.TIF   METHODMAN6_JALBERTINI.TIF

BERTINI.TIF   INSPECTADECK5_JALBERTINI.TIF   RAEKWON1_JALBERTINI.TIF   RAEKWON2_JALBERTINI.TIF   RAEKWON3_JALBERTINI.TIF

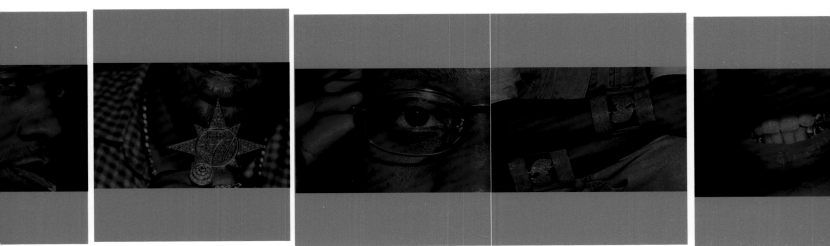

BERTINI.TIF   RZA_1_JALBERTINI.TIF   RZA_2_JALBERTINI.TIF   U_GOD_1_JALBERTINI.TIF   U_GOD_2_JALBERTINI.TIF

Grandmaster Flash

Bone Thugs-N-Harmony

A discovery of Eazy E, Bone Thugs-N-Harmony are one of the original groups to open up opportunities out in the Midwest. Seeing the lock East and West had on hip-hop, they got on a Greyhound and went to Ruthless Records to meet E. They returned to their post-industrial ghetto with a record deal. Easy-E was well known for using EPs as market testers and he did the same with his new Cleveland band. The result? "Thuggish Ruggish Bone" and "Tha Crossroads" hit hard. With their dream being realized, they turned the recording studio into a sweat shop and manufactured an effective first album, *E. 1999 Eternal*. Their fast rhymes and sinister harmonic wails can never be mastered by anyone except themselves. Them Bone Thugs could do a pro-life song about hospitals and brothers would be playin' it on their way to a drive by wit' loc'd out Gucci shades, sittin' on chrome! They made it cool for thugs to sing. When we first heard these cats, they scared the shit outta us! We gave 'em props for *Creepin' On Ah Come Up* and for holdin' down the top slot for over eight weeks. "1st of Tha Month" is the official anthem for low-rent development houses and trailer parks from New York to the dirty South. Respect goes out to the first family (outside the Death Row dynasty) to officially rep Thug Life in name and theory.

The Beat nuts

Hip - hop needs groups like this. At the time of this writing, to my knowledge, this Latin crew never went platinum. But they will. They've hit off so many artists in this Gaming Industry we call rap that the names wouldn't even fit on this page! Ju-Ju and Psycho Les are true hip-hop immortals. They will never stop because hip-hop is revolutionary, evolutionary, and necessary for children of all races, faces, and places. Respect these racketeers that have established one of the most successful two man production teams since Russell Simmons and Kurtis Blow's Orange Crush Prods. The Beatnut Junkies embody what this book is all about: Marketing, Consistency, Reach, Juice, and Style. In a word: GAME. For all the years they gave us, we are proud to hear them have the last word for they deserve to be the first served. God Bless Ju & Les.

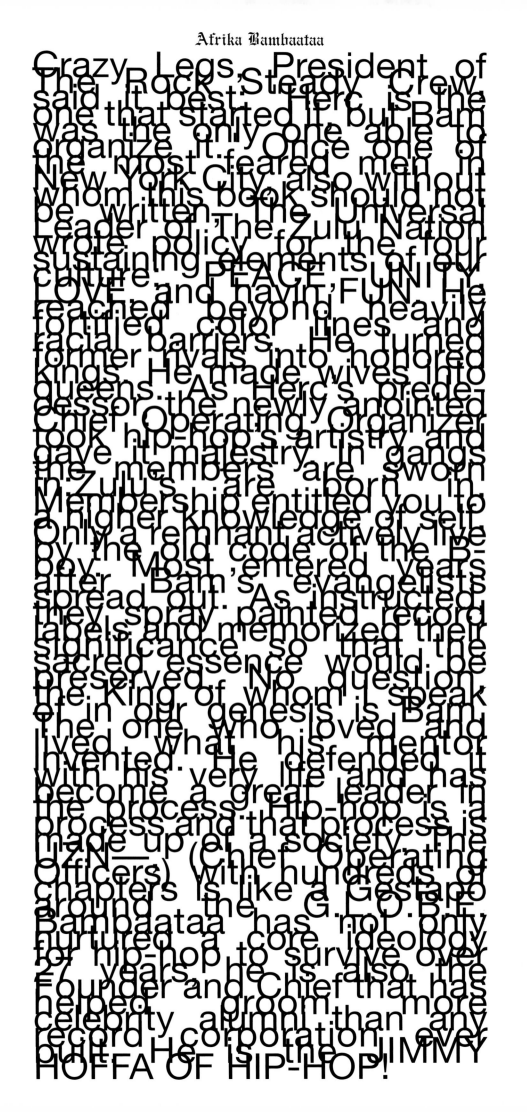

Afrika Bambaataa and The Soul Sonic Force

Fat Boys

Some thought they we
and the Gang, and—lik
The Fat Boys' blosso
early on as the Fresh
with the perception th
black, and rap. Sellin
after releasing six
immortality, but that w
cream sundae. The
(1985) blew them up
mainstream and with
fan favorite) these ov
continued to make a h
were the Fat Boys th
Disco Three. Prince
Robinson, and the lat
always been considere
Russell Simmons/ Ric
They were protecte
President Lyor Coh
group's royalties mak
could keep eating wel
"the bigger they com
"The Fat Boys" had a
will be remembered fo

inspired by Fat Albert
the Cosby creation—
ng popularity from as
st tour had much to do
t it was fun to be fat,
seven million records
lbums insures their
s just the tip of the ice
movie *Krush Groove*
into the commercial
987's *Disorderlies* (a
rweight heavyweights
ge splash. Before they
y were known as the
Markie Dee, Darren
Kool Rock 'Ski have
an integral part of the
Rubin Def Jam family.
by legendary Rush
n who guarded the
g sure the Fat Boys
Who was it that said,
the harder they fall?
ix-year run in rap that
ever.

Salt-N'-Pepa

These legendary ladies capitalized within a traditionally male-dominated thug sport becoming true-to-life hip-hop icons. Sandy "Pepa" Denton, Dee Dee Roper/Spinderella, and Cheryl "Salt" James busted out of the Sears Corporation where they worked with the underground hit "The Show Stopper," which challenged "The Show" by Slick Rick and Doug E. Fresh. Masterminded by their producer/manager Hurby Luv Bug, this was a traditional battle record that came with the eighties territory of 'Answer Records' and was enough to get them recognition and a deal on Next Plateau Records. Their debut album, Hot, Cool & Vicious in '87 included the three hip-hop immortals: "My Mic Sounds Nice," "Tramp," and "Chick on the Side." One of the biggest records of their careers, "Push It," is also one of the group's sexiest cuts and serves as a dare for anybody who claims to have staying power in and out of the studio! During the early Def Jam years, they could be seen shakin' that thang up on stage and every girl in the house wanted to look like them and every guy wanted.....well, let's just say that what they offered was Very Necessary. They contributed a string of chart hits—both on the pop and R&B lists—and became one of the first rap groups to be nominated for a Grammy for "Push It." They went on to win years later with "None of Your Business" in 995. Not only have they inspired nearly every female pop group that emerged after them but they also paved the way for an entire generation of women in music.

Money earnin' and reppin' Mount Vernon, DJ (and sometimes MC) Pete Rock was—and still is—one of the most talented and prolific producers hip-hop has ever spawned. And when Pete and the true Master of Ceremony, CL Smooth, found each other, it seemed like divine intervention. How else would you describe such majestical masterpiece singles "Mecca and the Soul Brother," "T.R.O.Y.," "Straighten it Out," or their 'shut you down' collabo with Run-D.M.C, "Down with the Kings." Words fail to properly express just how talented these two were and it is equally as hard to quantify their importance in this game. They elevated the entire art form.

The birth of hip-ho[p]
of old school con[...]
the   Cold   C[...]
Grandmaster. Ca[...]
Charlie Ch[...]
Kay-Gee,
were Bogg[...]
ends well?
Gang.
America's,
ry with.
Delight
immortalized on c[...]
the classic hip-hop[...]
Style. For a Hip-H[...]
taste of the real[...]
Pie, bite into *The C[...]*
Live In '82 and C[...]
Vs. The Fantastic[...]

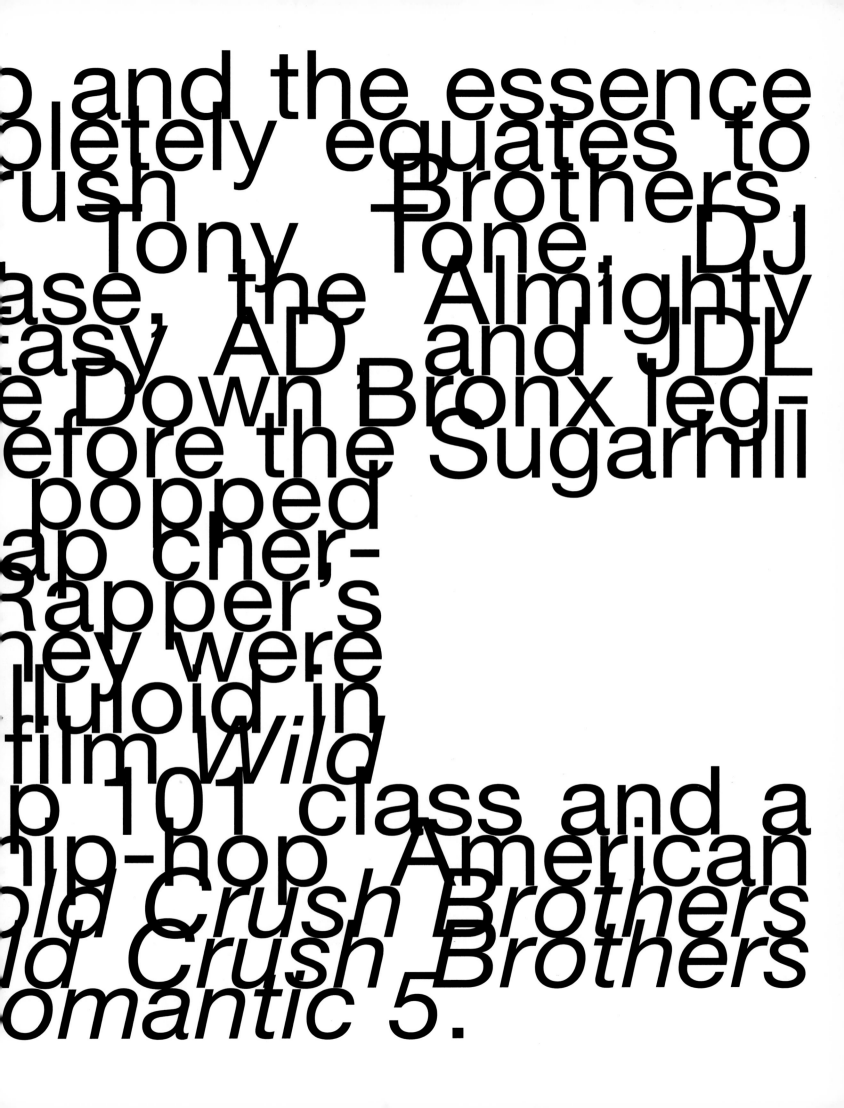

MANY A FOOL HAS TRIED TO FRONT ON THE HAMMER BUT THOSE WHO KNOW ANYTHING KNOW THAT HE WAS NOT LYING WHEN HE BOASTFULLY SNIPPED, "YOU CAN'T TOUCH THIS." FOR MOST OF THE LATE EIGHTIES AND EARLY NINETIES, MC HAMMER WAS VIRTUALLY UNTOUCHABLE AS HE SHIMMIED HIS WAY ACROSS AMERICA SELLING MORE ALBUMS THAN ANY OTHER RAP ACT IN HIP-HOP HISTORY. THE OAKLAND BORN STANLEY BURRELL MADE HIS MAJOR LABEL DEBUT IN 1988 WITH *LET'S GET IT STARTED*. "TURN THIS MUTHA OUT" INSTANTLY BECAME A PARTY FAVORITE AND THE ALBUM WENT ON TO SELL MILLIONS OF COPIES. SIMILAR TO *LET'S GET IT STARTED*, HIS FOLLOW-UP ALBUM, *PLEASE HAMMER DON'T HURT EM'*, HEAVILY SAMPLED THE WORKS OF P-FUNK, JAMES BROWN, AND MOST MEMORABLY RICK JAMES' "SUPERFREAK" ON THE HISTORIC SINGLE (AND HAMMER MOTTO), "U CAN'T TOUCH THIS." HAMMER WAS ALSO A BIG COVER ARTIST; REMAKING MANY CLASSIC HITS INCLUDING HIS SLOW, SIDE-STEPPING RENDITION OF THE CHI-LITES' "HAVE YOU SEEN HER?" *PLEASE HAMMER...* DISHED OUT ONE CHART-TOPPING SINGLE AFTER THE NEXT—INCLUDING THE RAPPING GOSPEL "PRAY"—AND EVENTUALLY WENT PLATINUM TEN TIMES OVER, BECOMING THE BEST SELLING RAP ALBUM OF ALL TIME. EVERY HIP-HOP IMMORTAL BRINGS SOMETHING UNIQUE TO THE TABLE AND WITH HAMMER IT WAS HIS HYPER-KINETIC, SHOW-STOPPING DANCE MOVES MADE ALL THE MORE FLAM-BOYANT BY HIS DECADENT BALLOON PANTS. THE VIBRANCY OF HAMMER'S SONGS IS ONLY PROPERLY TRANSLATED IN HIS LIVE SHOWS AND VIDEOS WHERE HE ALLOTTED PLENTY OF TIME TO FLEX THE FANCY FOOTWORK THAT MADE HIM FAMOUS. HIS SHOWS WERE WILD CIRCUSES WITH EXPLOSIONS AND TONS OF PEOPLE DANCING EVERYWHERE AS IF THE SPIRIT OF GOD HAD TAKEN HOLD OF THEIR FEET. HIS ELECTRIFYING STYLE IS SO INIMITABLE THAT HIS EXPERTISE REMAINS UNMATCHED. IN 1991 HIS SHUT UP HIS FEET AND LET HIS HANDS DO THE TALKING ON THE HUGELY POPULAR SINGLE "TOO LEGIT TOO QUIT," OFF HIS ALBUM OF THIS SAME NAME. THE FANCY HAND SIGNALS USED TO SIGN THE TITLE OF THE SONG QUICKLY BECAME A POP CULTURE PHENOMENON THAT REMAINED FRESH IN THE MEMORY OF HAMMER FANS MORE THAN A DECADE LATER. HE SAW ONLY ONE MORE HIT SINGLE WITH 1994'S "PUMP AND THE BUMP" FROM HIS FOURTH ALBUM, *THE FUNKY HEADHUNTER*; HAMMER'S GOLD-ALBUM TURN INTO THE GANGSTA RAP WORLD. ALTHOUGH HIS NEXT TWO ALBUMS WENT LARGELY UNNOTICED BY HIS FORMER FANS, THERE IS NO DENYING THE INVALUABLE CONTRIBUTIONS HE MADE TO HIP-HOP. HIS SUCCESS GREATLY CHANGED THE COURSE OF RAP MUSIC; MAKING IT MORE ACCESSIBLE TO THE PUBLIC AT LARGE AND ALL THE WHILE SHOWING US HOW TO TURN ANY PARTY OUT IN TRUE HAMMER STYLE.

DJ Jazzy Jeff & The Fresh Prince

William Smith III. He's clean-cut, full of jokes, and the pop/rap icon who received the parental seal of approval. Born and raised in Philly, at age 16 Smith met aspiring DJ Jeff Townes and together they dubbed themselves DJ Jazzy Jeff and The Fresh Prince. They soon became local stars with a bright future in music but they hit a snag when the Fresh Prince, upon high school graduation, was offered a scholarship to the highly-competitive university, M.I.T. After much contemplation, The Fresh Prince turned it down and chose to pursue his musical career. As shocking as his decision may have seemed, nobody in their right mind could have predicted the successes that lay ahead for Smith. In 1987, one year after graduation, the duo was signed to Jive Records and were, undoubtedly, the softest egg in a hair-boiled carton. The late eighties brought us hardcore singles such as "Fuck Tha Police" and "Fight the Power" which delivered extreme anti-establishment messages. Consequently, the hardcore fans weren't feeling his single, "Girls Aint Nothin' But Trouble"; a light weight, suburban approach laced with bubble-gum lyrics. But a whole new breed of hip-hop admirers was born. They delivered their sophomore effort, 1988's *He's the DJ; I'm the Rapper* (the first double album ever released from a rap artist), and the subsequent single, "Parents Just Don't Understand" which went into one of MTV's heaviest rotations. DJ Jazzy Jeff and the Fresh Prince had found their niche and secured it with the release of the classic and timeless sunny weather jam, "Summertime" off of 1991's *Homebase*. And that was just the beginning. And the beginning could very well be enough for the Fresh Prince to have earned his page in the book but he went on to do things that no black man in hip-hop, pop, or Hollywood had ever done. He segued his rap persona into the hit television show "The Fresh Prince of Bel Air" which had an impressive run of six years on prime-time television. The show was so strongly anchored around Will Smith's alter ego, 'The Fresh Prince,' that his decision to pursue a film career single-handedly ceased the shows production. His highly-acclaimed, dramatic portrayal of a gay con artist in his film debut, *Six Degrees of Separation*, hushed his harshest critics who, until then, hadn't taken Will's thespian efforts seriously. With the enormous success of *Independence Day* and *Men In Black* Smith became one of the first actors of any color to gain admittance into the ultra-exclusive 20 Million Dollar Club; joining the likes of Harrison Ford, Tom Cruise, Eddie Murphy, and Brad Pitt. And then in 2002 Smith became The first rapper ever nominated for an Academy Award for his portrayal of The Champ in *Ali*. Not content with being one of the highest paid movie stars in the world, Will initiated a solo career (sans Jazzy Jeff) in 1997 with the release of *Big Willie Style* and its 1999 multi-platinum follow-up *Willenium*. Call him soft, call him bubble-gum, call him whatever you want, Will Smith is a multitalented, dramatic and comedic genius of great depths who will always be Hollywood's Ghetto Golden Boy.

William Smith III. He's clean-cut, full of jokes, and the pop/rap icon who received the parental seal of approval. Born and raised in Philly, at age 16 Smith met aspiring DJ Jeff Townes and together they dubbed themselves DJ Jazzy Jeff and The Fresh Prince. They soon became local stars with a bright future in music but they hit a snag when the Fresh Prince, upon high school graduation, was offered a scholarship to the highly-competitive university, M.I.T. After much contemplation, The Fresh Prince turned it down and chose to pursue his musical career. As shocking as his decision may have seemed, nobody in their right mind could have predicted the successes that lay ahead for Smith. In 1987, one year after graduation, the duo was signed to Jive Records and were, undoubtedly, the softest egg in a hair-boiled carton. The late eighties brought us hardcore singles such as "Fuck Tha Police" and "Fight the Power" which delivered extreme anti-establishment messages. Consequently, the hardcore fans weren't feeling his single, "Girls Aint Nothin' But Trouble"; a light weight, suburban approach laced with bubble-gum lyrics. But a whole new breed of hip-hop admirers was born. They delivered their sophomore effort, 1988's *He's the DJ; I'm the Rapper* (the first double album ever released from a rap artist), and the subsequent single, "Parents Just Don't Understand" which went into one of MTV's heaviest rotations. DJ Jazzy Jeff and the Fresh Prince had found their niche and secured it with the release of the classic and timeless sunny weather jam, "Summertime" off of 1991's *Homebase*. And that was just the beginning. And the beginning could very well be enough for the Fresh Prince to have earned his page in the book but he went on to do things that no black man in hip-hop, pop, or Hollywood had ever done. He segued his rap persona into the hit television show "The Fresh Prince of Bel Air" which had an impressive run of six years on prime-time television. The show was so strongly anchored around Will Smith's alter ego, 'The Fresh Prince,' that his decision to pursue a film career single-handedly ceased the shows production. His highly-acclaimed, dramatic portrayal of a gay con artist in his film debut, *Six Degrees of Separation*, hushed his harshest critics who, until then, hadn't taken Will's thespian efforts seriously. With the enormous success of *Independence Day* and *Men In Black* Smith became one of the first actors of any color to gain admittance into the ultra-exclusive 20 Million Dollar Club; joining the likes of Harrison Ford, Tom Cruise, Eddie Murphy, and Brad Pitt. And then in 2002 Smith became The first rapper ever nominated for an Academy Award for his portrayal of The Champ in *Ali*. Not content with being one of the highest paid movie stars in the world, Will initiated a solo career (sans Jazzy Jeff) in 1997 with the release of *Big Willie Style* and its 1999 multi-platinum follow-up *Willenium*. Call him soft, call him bubble-gum, call him whatever you want, Will Smith is a multitalented, dramatic and comedic genius of great depths who will always be Hollywood's Ghetto Golden Boy.

(The above text is repeated numerous times in overlapping, faded layers across the page, then again clearly at the bottom:)

William Smith III. He's clean-cut, full of jokes, and the pop/rap icon who received the parental seal of approval. Born and raised in Philly, at age 16 Smith met aspiring DJ Jeff Townes and together they dubbed themselves DJ Jazzy Jeff and The Fresh Prince. They soon became local stars with a bright future in music but they hit a snag when the Fresh Prince, upon high school graduation, was offered a scholarship to the highly-competitive university, M.I.T. After much contemplation, The Fresh Prince turned it down and chose to pursue his musical career. As shocking as his decision may have seemed, nobody in their right mind could have predicted the successes that lay ahead for Smith. In 1987, one year after graduation, the duo was signed to Jive Records and were, undoubtedly, the softest egg in a hair-boiled carton. The late eighties brought us hardcore singles such as "Fuck Tha Police" and "Fight the Power" which delivered extreme anti-establishment messages. Consequently, the hardcore fans weren't feeling his single, "Girls Aint Nothin' But Trouble"; a light weight, suburban approach laced with bubble-gum lyrics. But a whole new breed of hip-hop admirers was born. They delivered their sophomore effort, 1988's *He's the DJ; I'm the Rapper* (the first double album ever released from a rap artist), and the subsequent single, "Parents Just Don't Understand" which went into one of MTV's heaviest rotations. DJ Jazzy Jeff and the Fresh Prince had found their niche and secured it with the release of the classic and timeless sunny weather jam, "Summertime" off of 1991's *Homebase*. And that was just the beginning. And the beginning could very well be enough for the

We referred to him as the interior designer of hip-house after hearing his 1988 platinum single, "It Takes Two." Rob Base and DJ E-Z Rock set fire to R & B charts, dancehalls, and radio sta- tions who had no choice but to familiarize themselves with this group. The single transcended every barri- er imaginable by deeply permeating the international club scene. Once it arrived, it set up shop. Any rapper or group that has records on retail in your local drugstore is immortal.

Tone Loc

With his huge h i t s of the late eighties and early nineties, "Funky Cold Medina," "Wild Thing," and "I Got It Goin' On," Tone Loc was part of the first wave of rappers to dominate the pop charts and cross over into the mainstream. His music became instantly recognizable because of his otherworldly b a r i t o n e v o i c e and his songs were on every play-list at Sadie Hawkins get-togethers and junior high dances across America. Although his musical career was short lived, Tone Loc made a lot of noise in a few short years and will always remain one of the most famous MCs in the world. You can't front on Loc.

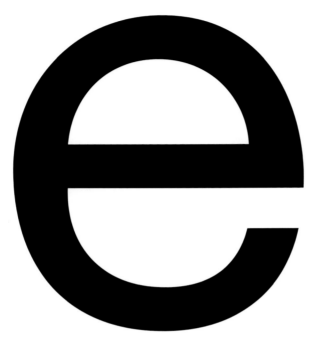

e

Eve

There is no disputing that Eve is one the best dressed and sexiest female MCs that hip-hop has ever seen. In less than two years she rightfully established herself as the style icon to emulate. But that is not why she is in this book. Like a pit bull attacking a Chihuahua, Eve gets on the mic and tears it up as she spits threats of domination and proclamations of superiority. All with probable cause. Eve Jihan Jeffers should have never asked us, "What Y'all Really Want?" because she's been telling us exactly what we're gonna get since she first blessed us with her lyrical presence on 1999's *Ryde or Die Volume 1*. In just a few very short years the First Lady of The Ruff Ryders made big contributions to hip-hop; ones that won't fade away when they leave heavy rotation. In 1998 she appeared on the *Bulworth* soundtrack and few people know it's her rapping on the Roots' classic 1999 single, "You Got Me" with Erykah Badu. In 2001 she collaborated with No Doubt's Gwen Stefani on "Let Me Blow Ya Mind" which was incidentally produced by Dr. Dre whose label failed to renew Eve's contract eventually leading to her deal with Ruff Ryders. The single ruled the airwaves much of 2001. That same year Eve confused us again when she asked, "Who's That Girl?," because we all knew it was the one with the pink or blonde or brown hair and those strategically located scratchy paw print tattoos that remind us of the fierceness that immortalized her from jump.

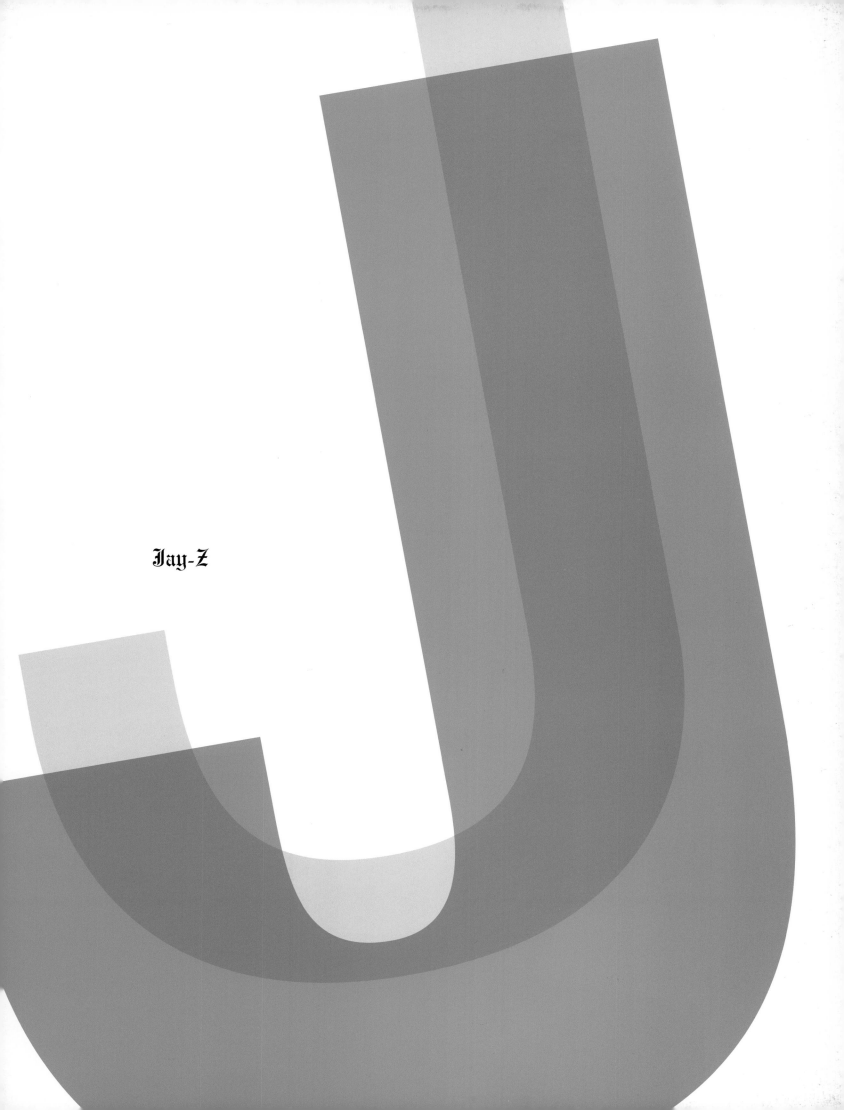

Jay-Z

here isn't an argument that could be crafted well enough to dispute he fact that Jay-Z is one of the best MCs to ever bless a mic. The man incapable of putting out a single or album that doesn't go platinum a azillion times over. Born Shawn Carter in the Brooklyn, NY Marcy rojects that his songs made infamous, Jay-Z was always destined for reatness. Before he was a great MC, he was a great hustler—a theme hat has been a common thread sewn throughout his music. He always ad hopes of making it big and in 1996—with business partners 'amon Dash and Kareem "Biggs" Burke—Jay released his debut lbum, *Reasonable Doubt,* on their independent label, Roc-A-Fella ecords. They landed a distribution deal with Priority and the album chieved a gold single with "Ain't No Nigga" (co-starring his female rotégé Foxy Brown). Although *Reasonable Doubt* embodied commer- ial viability, it failed to reach the mainstream. But Jay shot right back /ith 1997's *In My Lifetime, Vol. 1*, 1998's *Volume 2*, 1999's *Volume 3*, 000's *The Dynasty: Roc La Familia* and 2001's *Blueprint*. Do you see he pattern? Every year since he first came up, Jay-Z has released one nstoppable album after the next, dominating the hip-hop sector. lthough already firmly established and deeply admired, his massive reakthrough came with his fourth album, *Volume 3*, and more specif- :ally the single "Can I Get A…"— a playalistic battle of the sexes also tarring Amil and Ja Rule. No other rapper has consistently put out as nany hit singles as Jay-Z. Beginning in 1998, there was not a time vhen at least one (and usually two) of the heaviest rotated songs on the adio and MTV didn't belong to Jayhova: "The City Is Mine," "Can I Get \...," "Money, Cash, Hoes," "Hard Knock Life," "Jigga My Nigga," Nigga What, Nigga Who," "Do It Again," "Big Pimpin'," "I Just Wanna _ove You," and "HOVA." Legend has it that Jay doesn't write down nost of his lyrics but one person whose rhymes he did lay pen to paper or was Foxy Brown. Most of her biggest hits had Jigga behind the 2enmanship. His tales of hustlin', street life, drinking Cristal, and bling-)linging are so intricately woven that each time you listen to him it's a 1ew experience. Compound his impeccable rhyme style with his lyrical eferences— vaster than an encyclopedia—and you have one hip-hop)henomenon whose dynasty cannot be overthrown.

Kool G. Rap & D.J. Polo

Although he has been called a genius, he's never announced the "G" as such. We just' figured it was gangsta. Moe Dee disenfranchised the title of "Kool" as an official introduction for both DJ/rapper names forever. We call this man *G-Rap*. He's the Al Capone of crime storytelling. If James Cagney ever touched a mic, he'd quit when G-rap walked in. A lot of suckers did. Hiz lyrical delivery in a battle was like watching a pitbull maul a small child. After him and Polo (hiz DJ) met through Eric B.; their chief objective became eliminating competitors. In 1989 they marked their turf with a 12inch blast, "It's a Demo," letting family heads know the underbelly must be fed. "Road To Riches" showed the possibilities of unifying disorganized rhyme. *Wanted Dead or Alive* said, as racketeers, they would be outlaws in the industry but in 1992 the yellow line was drawn down Tuph St. It said time was up! Get on or get out! If I respect you, we'll agree to divide the market into separate territorial monopolies. If not, then expect to get blown out the frame. The result: Fat Crack: TS, Mobb Deep, Mash Out Posse, Raekwon The Chef, Heavy D & his Boyz, and the Funk Master all held the line along side him. A representative from each of the five families helped pour the cement for hiz boots that still stand tall on the walk of fame.

Too $hort

He's inspired virtually every playa, balla, hustler, and pimp daddy mack in this game. Just ask Ice-T, Ant Banks, 8 Ball & MJG, Jay-Z, Scarface, and E-40. A true legend coming straight out of the Bay area; hip-hop immortality began for Todd Shaw in the early eighties when he was selling his 90 minute cassettes (*Players* and *Don't Stop Rappin'*) out of the trunk of his car. He was one of the first rappers to use the term dog and he also holds the patent for the splendid term 'beeeyitch'—a catchy variation of *bitch*. Each city has its grapevine—a way to get the skinny on the street. Too $hort innovated the Oakland grapevine as it was the only way you could find out about his joints. Nearly twenty years later he's released twelve albums spawning no less than fifteen West Coast branded classics including: "Life Is Too Short," "Short but Funky," "Freaky Tales," "Pimp Shit," and "I'm A Player." His music has pushed millions and millions of units despite the big-budget marketing, advertising, and MTV promoting ploys that are absolutely essential to the success of any new artist today. Too $hort retired from solo recordings in 1996 at the age of thirty leaving millions of his admirers stunned and heartbroken. Three years later he came back with *Can't Stay Away* gratifying fans on the East Coast, West Coast, and everywhere in between.

EPMD

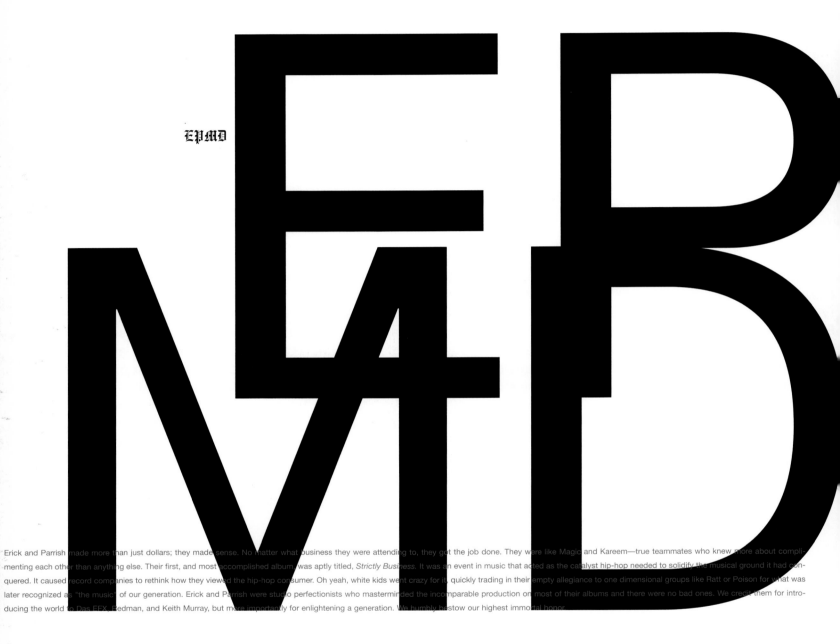

Erick and Parrish made more than just dollars; they made sense. No matter what business they were attending to, they got the job done. They were like Magic and Kareem—true teammates who knew more about complimenting each other than anything else. Their first, and most accomplished album, was aptly titled, *Strictly Business*. It was an event in music that acted as the catalyst hip-hop needed to solidify the musical ground it had conquered. It caused record companies to rethink how they viewed the hip-hop consumer. Oh yeah, white kids went crazy for it, quickly trading in their empty allegiance to one dimensional groups like Ratt or Poison for what was later recognized as "the music" of our generation. Erick and Parrish were studio perfectionists who masterminded the incomparable production on most of their albums and there were no bad ones. We credit them for introducing the world to Das EFX, Redman, and Keith Murray, but more importantly for enlightening a generation. We humbly bestow our highest immortal honor.

Coolio

Coolio is the perfect name for this brother. He is hella kool, but his address is no joke. The millionaire native of Compton, CA, debuted in 1994 with *It Takes A Thief*— made platinum by the P-Funk, "Fantastic Voyage." Back East we heard it and dug it without question. You couldn't turn on the radio and miss it. Coolio held it down again in 1995 with the song that made him an immortal: "Gangsta's Paradise." I've seen thugz become reflective and even remorseful over this super hit. It made such an impact within the community, trust me, play it today and I swear you'll nod your head and do a two step or sumphin' for the first twelve seconds, then forget about dancing and start thinking about your homies that got moked. It will leave you stuck. It won a Grammy in 1996 and the crowd went crazy. After that every studio wanted Coolio on the record. Soundtrack offers were pouring in. It would be inappropriate not to mention him.

Public Enemy

I don't know if it was Lyor Cohen or Khalid Muhammad who stepped to this tag team first but whomever encouraged the unifying force of a graphic artist (Chuck D) and a trained classical pianist (Flavor Flav) to organize rap's most revolutionary group, helped save hip-hop at a critical time in rap's history! Takin' the James Cagney film title to the Apollo, Public Enemy#1 brought the boycott with *Yo! Bum Rush the Show* in 1987. Only those who had direct dealings with Def Jam knew who The Bomb Squad was. Eric Sadler, Keith & Hank Shocklee are the legendary producers of seven albums that will live on in infamy. "Miuzi Weighs a Ton" scared the livin' shit out of me! My whole block would stand around the radio in terror. That song made us invest in a lot of iron. Jams quickly ceased due to being shot up. We were real stupid then. We never considered the warning that Chuck D and his innovative side kick—an addicted wild ass midget with a black top hat and a 'made in china' clock around his neck—were delivering. The word was out on the street that an album had dropped that had some whyle kids on the cover, killing a DJ in the middle of a tune. Twelve months later, *It Takes A Nation of Millions to Hold Us Back* was the official day of reckoning in the rap world. Their threats were real and that midget was fit to be tied on stage. With the most powerful independent label under their belts, Terminator X on the wheels of reels, and what looked like Naval Officers or a black faction of the Guardian Angels holdin' down the set (The S.1.W), they were the Untouchables! Under the leadership of Chuck D, the modern day Malcolm X of hip-hop (ironically, *The Autobiography of Malcolm X* is the first reference made of hip-hop as entity within) another masterful production by the expensive Bomb Squad—it was clear what that image on their first album cover meant. No more music by the suckers and the suckers were any and all who weren't pro-rap. PROGRESSIVE RAP. I don't know them as individuals so, I can only comment on significance. Chuck, Griff, X, and Flav are educated men who hold degrees speaking on Farrakhan and socialism, class distinction, racism, fascism, and niggerism in a mannerism that bullwhipped our society and its hated black stereotypes. I'm sure they, and many politicians and activists, wouldn't have cared much if Public Enemy was advocating a more contemporary kind of entertainment unlike "Black Steel In The Hour Of Chaos" or "Don't Believe The Hype"— a well deserved all out assault on hack journalists who hate our music and the fact that it employs even those who love it. They were the most important rap group since Afrika Bambaataa and The Soul Sonic Force. That's why they are still, after thirteen years, the only group to earn three consecutive five star albums and a four and a half for *Bum Rush.* Dig it. That's 19 & 1/2 stars, on four albums, in five years. That's immortality at a time when every MC was a dealer or a user, even Flavor Flav, but back then who wasn't? They pioneered a pilgrimage for power building. Made brothers go from crack to kufi's in jus' one hit. The real slap in the face is that after all that was achieved, brothers traded in those red, black, and greens for diamonds and crystal glasses of Champale choosing acceptance over respect—what Malcolm warned about when he MC'd the bum rush. The Anti-Nigger Machine, B.K.A. Prophets Of Rage, the most dangerous rap group in the world! They had gold singles and platinum albums on every wall in the office, their phones were tapped, had death threats from anti-terrorist groups, and labeled communists. The Enemy struck much more than black, it struck a cord in suburban homes and headquarters of the FBI and CIA. With gangster rap gaining a strangle hold on the industry, P.E. didn't just push the envelope, they mailed the letter! Volatile times call for sacrifice, rebels for a cause, and air-raihistoric entertainment.

People either love him or hate him but whichever way they may feel there is no denying the vast and invaluable contributions Puffy has made to hip-hop. The careers of Mary J. Blige, Biggie Smalls, Craig Mack, Jodeci and countless

P. Diddy

others have his fingerprints all over them. It took him mere months to go from intern to Vice President of A&R at Uptown Records answering directly to Andre Harrell. When Andre bitterly let Puffy go he repaid the gesture by starting Bad

Boy Records and eventually hiring his old boss to work for him. Perhaps the greatest thing Puffy ever did (besides dating Jennifer Lopez) was signing Biggie Smalls and producing his debut, *Ready to Die*—one of the greatest rap album

ever made. It seems the Mogul/Ceo/Producer titles weren't enough for Puffy so he went out and made his own album, *No Way Out*, which was released in 1997, just months after the death of his protégé Biggie Smalls. He's not th

greatest rapper in the world but he is one of the best entertainers; when it comes to his own music he has the perfect knack for recycling old songs and turning them into number one hits—one after another after another. Puffy owns t

patent to the term 'ghetto fabulous' and his extravagant lifestyle

—Bentleys, yachts, Cristal, and million-dollar pendants—

set the stage for a whole new breed of young MCs. After dominating much of the rap industry in the late nineties, Puffy expanded his entr

preneurial horizons when he launched his own clothing line, Sean John. It wasn't long before his signature line was raking in hundreds of millions of dollars in sales as the premier choice of clothing for young urbanites. The new mille

nium saw the exasperated success of teeny boppers acts and one of the top charters was Puffy's own girl group, Dream—a brave and lucrative step away from his rap roots. In 2001, after the highly publicized break-up of his relation

ship with J. Lo and his subsequent acquittal of gun charges stemming from a 1999 altercation at Club USA, Puffy released a press statement in the form of a hit single, "Bad Boy For Life." The hook repeatedly told us Puffy wasn't goin

anywere and we understood the message but don't be misled—Puffy—the restauranteur, designer, rapper, producer, everyman— is, in fact, always going somewhere—it just happens to be far beyond any of his competitors.

The Fugees

The Fugees' debut, *Blunted on Reality*, lent credibility to Gang Starr's catch phrase, "Hard to Earn"—particularly because the Fugees were never a hard-core group. Their formula was sim-ple—to make well produced songs with the help of Chris Schwartz and Joe the Butcher of Ruffhouse. But the secret to their suc-cess was their wise decision to make songs that were familiar to the baby boomers. *The Score* made their first album look—and sell—like a lead pipe. It put a nickel on their needle. After five million albums on top of the belt-drive, critics wanted to know how and why. I was at a show of theirs and was stunned when L-Boogie started to sing. I was like, 'What the hell is she doin'?!' No female MC can hang with her. Period. Her brothers in the industry can't step in her arena. Wyclef Jean is a straight up B-Boy! You can put his love for the cul-ture next to the giants and it will stand the test. Pras too. The only test it couldn't stand was success as a group. Lauryn Hill got differ-ent love on stage because she was the shorty. A shorty who could spit, sing, and swing like nothing in our past. She went on to become the first rapper to hold the cover of *Time* magazine and win five Grammys for her solo debut, *The Miseducation of Lauryn Hill*. Wyclef's solo career took off in 1997 when he released *The Carnival* and the

Stay
Alive.

Heavy D

Heavy D

For years we've affectionately called him 'The Overweight Lover' but you can also call him a legend. Raised in Money Earnin' Mount Vernon, Big Heav started freestyling at the tender age of eight. While in high school he banged $1,500 out of a casino in Atlantic City, bought a drum machine, then hooked up with his man DJ Eddie F and went for broke. He went on to sign with Andre Harrell's Uptown Records and in 1986 Heavy D & The Boyz (DJ Eddie F and G Wiz) released their first album, *Livin' Large,* which went on to sell over 500,000 copies (an unprecedented number for that time) and spawned two infectious hip-hop classics "Mr. Big Stuff" and "The Overweight Lover's In The House." Since then he's braced six more albums: *Big Tyme, Peaceful Journey, Blue Funk, Nuttin' But Love, Waterbed,* and *Heavy* amassing sales of more than four million albums. When Heavy shows up anywhere it's as if the President has walked into the Oval Office. His presence and respect for business are nothing less than professional. He's been a balla for years now and his rep- utation is sterling in and out of the industry. He's as graceful as Jackie Gleason in all his zoot suit videos. Take it from Malone, whether at a table with Eddie F or in a trailer with Eddie Murphy, he's a big shot who has made his bones.

ICE-T

Sadly enough, Tracy Morrow's parents died before they could see their son go on to become one of hip-hop's most important and powerful figures. A New Jersey native, Morrow relocated to South Central Los Angeles in the late seventies after his parent's fatal car crash. He instantly took to the West Coast hip-hop scene while a student at Crenshaw High School. Out of respect for his hero, the notorious pimp and author Iceberg Slim, he took the name Ice-T and, at once, a legend was born. By the time he made his LP debut, Ice-T was already a seasoned vet having released numerous 12 inch singles (including "Body Rock" and "The Coldest Rap" and appearing in such hip-hop films as *Breakin' II: Electric Boogaloo*. He debuted with *Rhyme Pays* in 1987 and that same year he penned and performed the title track for Dennis Hopper's classic cop drama, *Colors*. "I am a nightmare walking, psychopath talking…" was the first verse of a perfectly written, unnerving narrative of LA gang life. Two hip-hop albums later, in 1992, Ice-T collaborated with his heavy metal band, Body Count, to release their self-titled debut and the one single that would change his life forever, "Cop Killer." Overnight, Ice-T became the target of the NRA and every right-wing group (and a few left) in the nation, simultaneously thrusting Ice-T into the media spotlight. He addressed his accusers with piercing intellect and poignant rebuttals. Throughout the nineties, Ice-T would alternate between head-banger, pimped out rapper, social commentator, and budding thespian. He appeared in the 1991 classic *New Jack City* and since the eighties has appeared in over fifty movies, documentaries, and specials including the hilarious HBO documentary *Pimps Up, Hoes Down* in which Ice-T—in a true testament to his pimp and hustler roots—made an appearance at the annual Player's Ball in Las Vegas. More than most other artists, Ice-T had used hip-hop as his rallying call to bring attention to the many social injustices suffered by black people. His career constantly endured but it is because Ice-T is not just a rapper, he is a survivor.

cold crush 4 ramell & shockdell rodney e cheeba eddie ed busy b lisa lee sha roc pebblie poo lil r

rodney e cheeba eddie ed busy b lisa

busy b lisa le

lisalisalisalisali

...na roc

...bblie poo lil markie c colc

...alisalisa li

lisalisalisa

lisa

lisalisalisa

busy b lisa lee sha roc pebblie

...salisa lis

lisalisalisalisalisalisalisalisalisalisalisalisalisalisali

lisalisalisalisalisalis

...o lil markie c cold crush 4 ramell & s

lisalisalisalisa

...ckdell rodney e cheeba e

lisalisalisa

lisalisalisalisa

salisalisalisa

poo lil markie c cold c

ramell & shockdell rodney e cheeba eddie ed busy b lisa lee

cheeba eddie ed busy b lisa lee sha roc pebblie poo lil markie c cold crush 4 ramell & shockdell r

sha roc pebblie poo lil markie c cold crush 4 ramell & shockdell rodney e cheeba eddie ed busy b

cold crush 4 ramell & shockdell rodney e cheeba eddie ed busy b lisa lee sha roc pebblie poo lil

rodney e cheeba eddie ed busy b lisa lee sha roc pebblie poo lil markie c cold crush 4 ramell & si

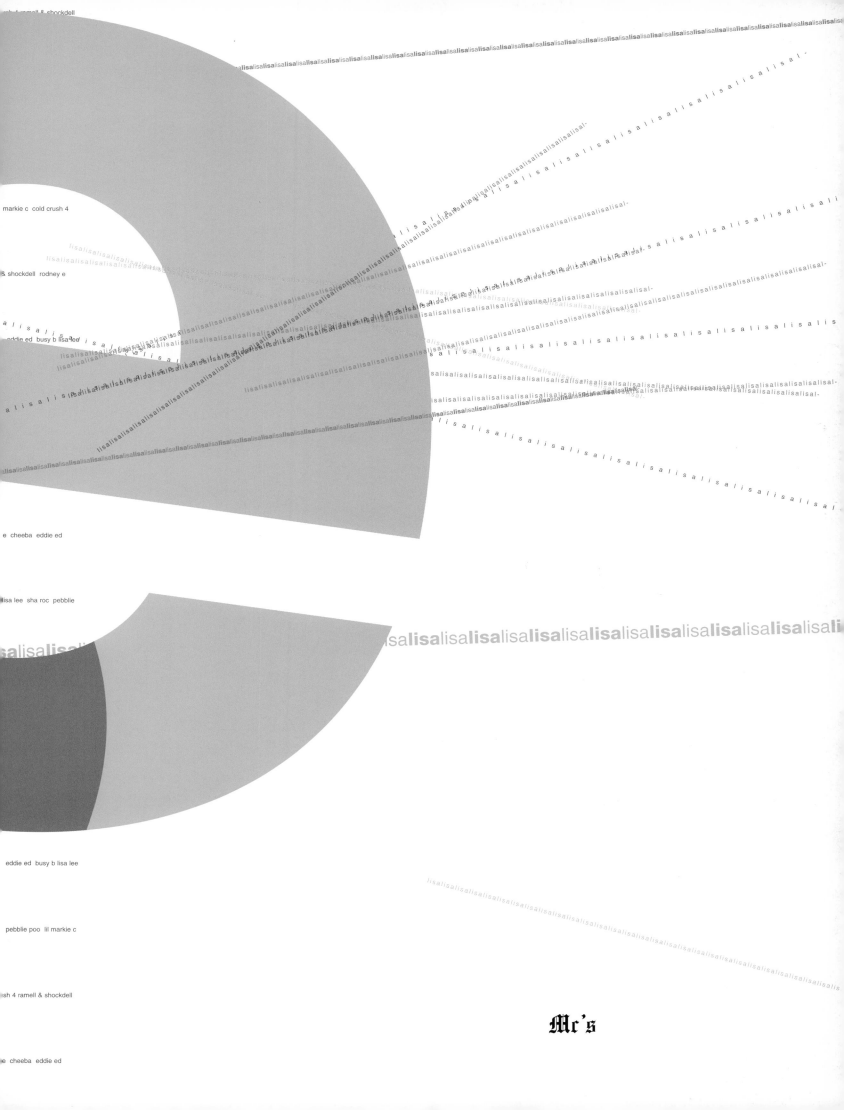

sh 4 ramell & shockdell

markie c cold crush 4

& shockdell rodney e

eddie ed busy b lisa lee

e cheeba eddie ed

lisa lee sha roc pebblie

eddie ed busy b lisa lee

pebblie poo lil markie c

sh 4 ramell & shockdell

e cheeba eddie ed

Mc's

THIS IS FOR LA RAZA

Lauryn Hill

She is the one that educated a nation about the misunderstanding of what the flamboyant culture is not, while at the same time plat-forming for what it could be. If y'all have never heard her pull her skirt down and show some shorts on the mic, then y'all don't know the power of Lauryn Hill. L Boogie is one of the very best MCs we've ever heard do it. Her solo debut, *The Miseducation of Lauryn Hill*, is the only album that perfectly combines all musical influences and blends them into a perfect ten figure elixir made for the mind to drink. Her vision of the city spinning on a turntable (brought to life by the skilled video director Sanji) is the best hip-hop video I've ever seen. If she ever decides it's time to show her ass again, the lethal MC and hip-hop icon would have every rapper in the world on one knee for a chance to sit next to her chair. L Boogie: eternal talent.

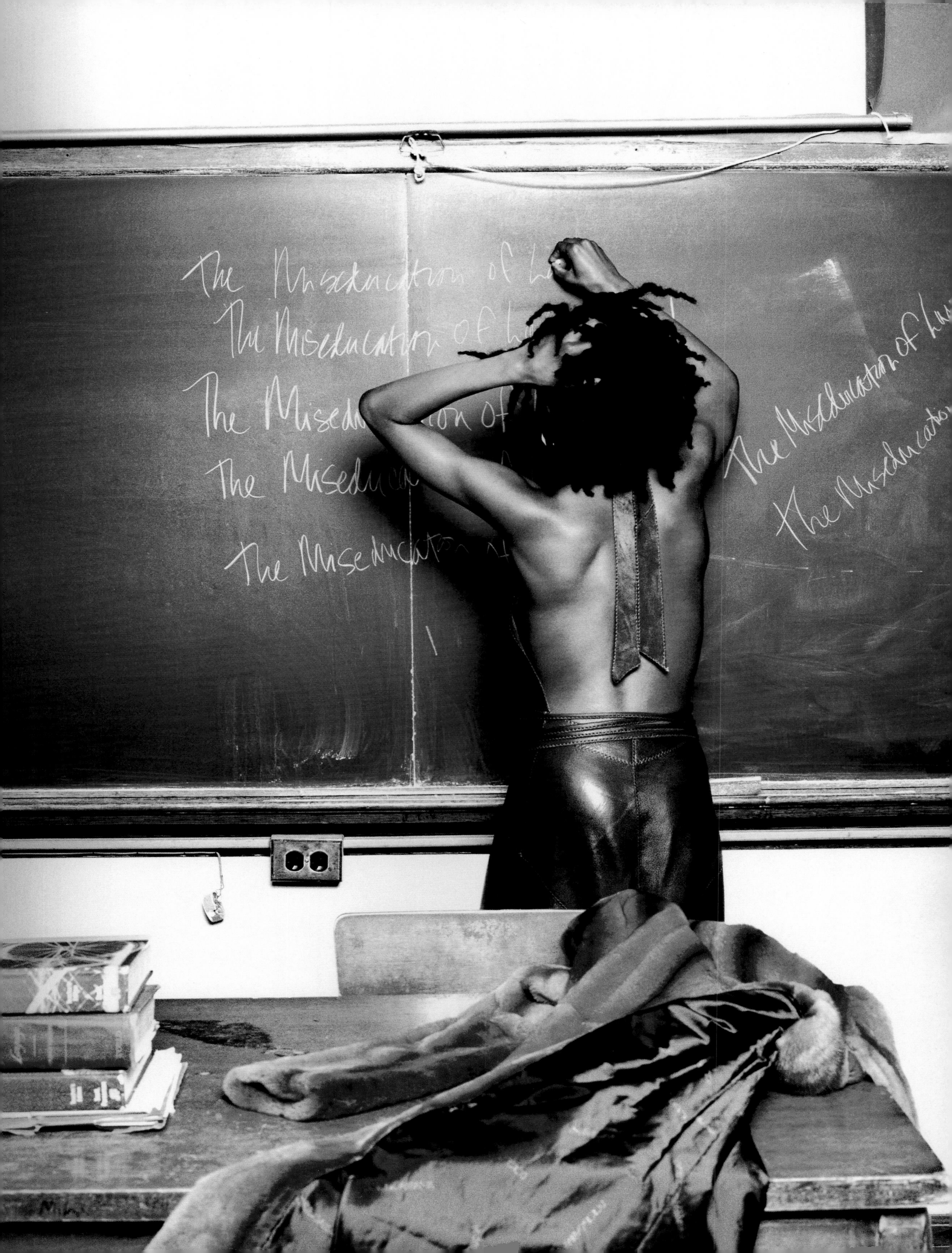

ice cube

Before Eminem there was N.W.A.'s most controversial offspring, Ice Cube. In the mid-eighties Ice Cube penned the lyrics to the hugely famous gangster anthem, "Boyz N Da Hood" which was originally rejected by Eazy-E and his cre
HBO, but eventually found its way onto N.W.A.'s debut album, *N.W.A. and the Posse*. In 1989, after just one LP, Ice Cube left N.W.A. but was quick to forge a solo career. He released his monumental debut album, *Amerikka's Most Wante*
in 1990 and became one of the first West Coast rappers to team up with an East Coast production team—The Bomb Squad of Public Enemy's camp. Cube immediately tore up the scene. As a solo artist, his superiorly intelligent politi
commentary greatly set him apart from his peers and his angry and controversial lyrics garnered him millions of adoring fans. Ice Cube's voice is a battle horn in the game and, besides Snoop Dogg, he is the only other living MC from
days of Death Row that has held on to the secret recipe for making every single a platinum one. He has released six solo albums since 1991 and each and every one has not only gone gold or platinum but has spawned timeless singl
that will be played on the radio and in clubs for decades to come. "It Was A Good Day," "Check Yo Self," and "Steady Mobbin'" are a few of Cube's perfect contributions to his immortality. His Priority catalog is a collector's pride and a
real rap connoisseur would have *Death Certificate* (1991) in their collection. In addition to his contributions with the Westside Connection—a group he helped from in 1996 with Mack 10 and WC—Cube also masterminded the career of
West Coast gangsterette Yo-Yo. Ice Cube also seems to be one of the only living MCs who holds the secret recipe for rapper-to-actor crossover. As much as he is recognized for his angry and intimidating rhymesaying; he is just as famo
if not more, for his numerous movie roles and film accomplishments. No one will ever forget his turn as the hard-core-gangster Doughboy in *Boyz 'N' Da Hood* (1991). He then went on to write and produce both *Friday* and *Next Friday* wh
grossed over ninety million dollars collectively. Cube is a true inspiration, not just for surviving some real hectic times but also because he innovated his game while layin' low. He is as big or as little as he wants to be but he never makes
big deal out of his life. He does things his way, he always has and he always will.

DJ Quik

Known as one of the most slept on producers in the game; Quik first dropped his Cali gheri curl juice on wax back in the late eighties with heavy funk influence. Quik was wise beyond his years. He was successful at marketing himself slowly, avoiding saturating the market which allowed him to remain in demand. Commissioning a track by this man is a grip. Quik don't come cheap. Deborah Cox, AMG, The Watts Prophets, and even Shaquille O'Neal stood in line for his dunkin' donuts. Still down with the Dogg Pound special producers unit; he remains a go-to-man since before "Murder Was The Case." Destined for the hall of fame, Quik can retire his jersey any day he wants.

courtesty of the writers' bench

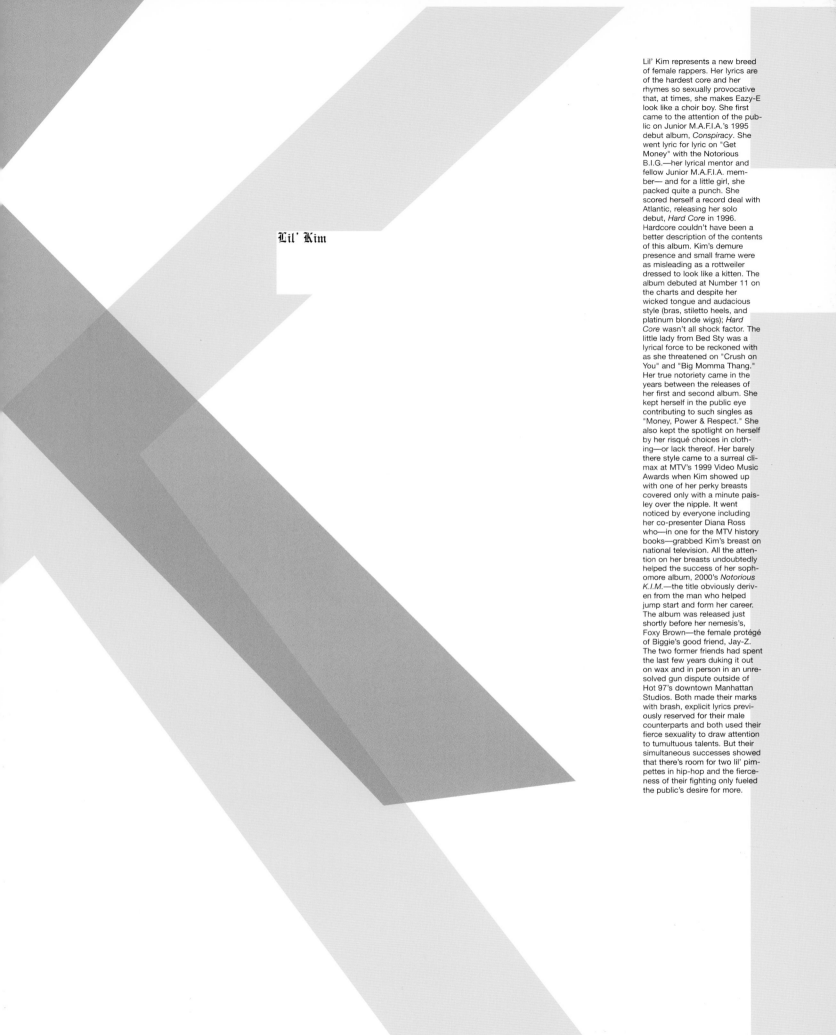

Lil' Kim

Lil' Kim represents a new breed
of female rappers. Her lyrics are
of the hardest core and her
rhymes so sexually provocative
that, at times, she makes Eazy-E
look like a choir boy. She first
came to the attention of the public on Junior M.A.F.I.A.'s 1995
debut album, *Conspiracy*. She
went lyric for lyric on "Get
Money" with the Notorious
B.I.G.—her lyrical mentor and
fellow— Junior M.A.F.I.A. member— and for a little girl, she
packed quite a punch. She
scored herself a record deal with
Atlantic, releasing her solo
debut, *Hard Core* in 1996.
Hardcore couldn't have been a
better description of the contents
of this album. Kim's demure
presence and small frame were
as misleading as a rottweiler
dressed to look like a kitten. The
album debuted at Number 11 on
the charts and despite her
wicked tongue and audacious
style (bras, stiletto heels, and
platinum blonde wigs); *Hard
Core* wasn't all shock factor. The
little lady from Bed Sty was a
lyrical force to be reckoned with
as she threatened on "Crush on
You" and "Big Momma Thang."
Her true notoriety came in the
years between the releases of
her first and second album. She
kept herself in the public eye
contributing to such singles as
"Money, Power & Respect." She
also kept the spotlight on herself
by her risqué choices in clothing—or lack thereof. Her barely
there style came to a surreal cli-
max at MTV's 1999 Video Music
Awards when Kim showed up
with one of her perky breasts
covered only with a minute pais-
ley over the nipple. It went
noticed by everyone including
her co-presenter Diana Ross
who—in one for the MTV history
books—grabbed Kim's breast on
national television. All the attention on her breasts undoubtedly
helped the success of her sophomore album, 2000's *Notorious
K.I.M.*—the title obviously deriv-
en from the man who helped
jump start and form her career.
The album was released just
shortly before her nemesis's,
Foxy Brown—the female protégé
of Biggie's good friend, Jay-Z.
The two former friends had spent
the last few years duking it out
on wax and in person in an unre-
solved gun dispute outside of
Hot 97's downtown Manhattan
Studios. Both made their marks
with brash, explicit lyrics previously reserved for their male
counterparts and both used their
fierce sexuality to draw attention
to tumultuous talents. But their
simultaneous successes showed
that there's room for two lil' pim-
pettes in hip-hop and the fierceness of their fighting only fueled
the public's desire for more.

KID CAPRI KID CAPRI KID CAPRI KID CAPRI KID CAPRI KID CAPRI BRUCIE B BRUCIE B BRUCIE B BRUCIE B BRUCIE B BRUCIE B BRUCIE B DJ CLUE DJ CLUE DJ CLUE DJ CLUE DJ CLUE DJ CLUE DJ CLUE BATTLECAT BATTLECAT BATTLECAT BATTLECAT BATTLECAT BATTL
DJ PREMIERE DJ PREMIERE DJ PREMIERE DJ PREMIERE DJ PREMIERE DJ POLO DJ POLO DJ POLO DJ POLO DJ POLO DJ POLO DJ POLO DJ RED ALERT DJ RED ALERT DJ RED ALERT DJ RED ALERT DJ RED ALERT MARLEY MARL MARLEY MARL MARLEY MARL MARLEY MARL MARLEY MARL M

The job of the DJ is of paramount importance. He or she sets the tone and the timing for the overture like a maestro before a thousand musicians. In the streets, they brushed their Pumas as often as they brushed their waves or tapered their pant legs. You were/ are those thousand musicians listening for the break. The improvisations are yours to blend, scratch, and cut with other limitless antiques. Just be discrete. Critics that exposed the origins of well-disguised samples that DJs used were cursed out, blacklisted, had contracts put out on them, and eventually got walked up on and stuffed. You can understand it's about keepin' the Koad of Silence. Just because you've got a fat advance to do an album doesn't mean you want to spend your money payin' for other people's recordz. Before the death of disco and afta the S.O.S. Bands, the Ohio Players' "Take Your Time" and "Roller Coaster" got butchered by the novice; future producers advanced their skills on Paul Winleys' "Super Disco Breaks." His limited editions featured "Marti Gras" by Bob James, Jimmy Bohern's "Spank," and one of The Grand Wizard's favorites, "Paradise." Then came *Ultimate Break Beats* with "Funky Chicken," "Daisy Lady," "The Drummers Beat" by Herman Kelly, "Theme from S.W.A.T.," " Get Up And Dance," "Impeach The President," and the unforgettable "Hand Clapping Song." Every hip-hop classic ever made was inspired by these trophies and the men and women who polished them for the crowd. The immortal James Brown was played so much that it was virtually impossible to find a unique way of using his lithogram for anyone's recordz. Ganksta Boogie didn't happen until all the known breaks were mastered effortlessly. The street DJs had to get more creative and come up out of their "nigga bag" with new shit. They reached for Devo, Kraftwerk, Steve Miller Band, Hall and Oats, Led Zep, and even Queen for the C.R.E.A.M. Yet, again it was Flash that introduced the Beat Box as a secret weapon for the extra drum and bass at the battle. Ever since Beat Box was done live by him, it has been an instrumental part of the music and its progression of hip-hop culture. The SP Series is a staple that's been used to produce and reproduce beats that keep other people from charging extortion prices for the use of their original drum loops. I don't remember the piece of shit Flash played with to set the ball in motion, but there isn't anyone who has knowledge of producing and hasn't an SP 12, which eventually became SP 1200 (the beginner's tool for aspiring producers for over twenty years). It's what Milk & Giz tricked out to score "Top Billin'." Howie Tee wouldn't have been able to break his artist in a big way without it. You think DJ Scratch was bangin' his hand against the lunch table for "Strictly Business?" Stop Playin?!! It's what Ant Banks and Mark the 45 King stole for Christmas. Prince Paul and Jermaine Dupri had their labels write off for 'em. Get the picture? Next came the MPC 60 with hollow kicks and that warm, waxed, plastic drum stuffed with moving carpet noize. The style of equipment Pete Rock kept under his pillow havin' wet dreams about the soulful sounds he was going to make the next morning. For the 3000 you'd have to call Timbaland or Teddy Riley, who would bring his latest trophies into the crack infested park of St. Nicolas. The 2000 and 2000XL took care of everybody from DJ Quik to The Abbot of Shaolin (RZA), E-40 to De La Soul's third album. For some, it almost became more important to keep up with the technology than the imagery of the DJ and her trademark coffin with headphones. When Flash introduced the machine he had already "Grandmastered" it. Holding to everlasting code competitive sportsmanship, he created phat beats that wouldn't be duplicated in time to lose the Champale prize because they

LOVEBUG STARSKI LOVEBUG STARSKI LOVEBUG STARSKI LOVEBUG STARSKI DJ MARK THE 45 KING DJ MARK THE 45 KING DJ MARK THE 45 KING TIMBALAND TIMBALAND TIMBALAND TIMBALAND TIMBALAND PRINCE PAUL PRINCE PAUL PRINCE PAUL PRINCE PAUL PRINCE FUNKMASTER FLEX FUNKMASTER FLEX FUNKMASTER FLEX FUNKMASTER FLEX RZA RZA RZA RZA RZA RZA RZA RZA RZA RZA MR. MAGIC MR. MAGIC MR. MAGIC MR. MAGIC MR. MAGIC MR. MAGIC DOMINO DOMINO DOMINO DOMINO DOMINO DOMINO DOMINO

were made on the spot. Every famous DJ and professional producer understands that their contributions will be infringed upon and straight up jacked by wannabe Hit Men. Just like Mickey Mouse when he broke the broomstick in *Fantasia* and created a thousand little street sweepers in the ears and eyes of the thousand musicians. Here are a few names of those who were payin' more than their share of dues in the schoolyard. They were payin' attention to the future of electronic percussion and its strangle hold on other people's rap recordz. ASR keyboards became the version to control soon afta. It allowed a greater selection of sounds to be duplicated, tracks to be recorded simultaneously, and few other tricks that anything but a human beat box could battle.

Today, you ain't sayin' nuthin' if you're not workin' with the best in the bizniz. Kurzwerl, Trinity, and the Triton are for ballerz strictly on that Producer Of The Year status. But not all legendary DJs have left the park! Some of them don't own or operate heavy machinery other than the black SL-1210's and matching mixer. They have no adhesive tape on any of their vintage vinyls. The records are covered with graffiti. One look at the little red light and you are pulled into the Cerwin-Vega's and pushed around by the crossfader. These aristocrats would start a block party with "Last Night Changed It All" and end the night with "It's Great to Be Here." Like DJ Hollywood, who has been puttin' it down for over thirty years without a record! Or Chuck Chillout who started out

as Red Alert's record man and filled in for him on his radio show, establishing himself as a present legend. Cash Money who won the 1989 DMC championship with Bounce, Rock, and Skate. Jazzy Joyce is in a class by herself and it's not because she's one of the last original female DJs, but due to her continual professionalism throughout her career. Unlike most DJs who act like impatient fans, Jazzy Joyce never bitched and moaned when the spotlight wasn't on her. She always acted as if it were on her and it's never left her in the darkness. And Kid Capri, The Original Black Italian and the most recognized Street DJ in the world. His 52 Beats are better than Theodore's 100 beats, in both quality and pace. He proved to be a hip-hop icon like his

predecessor, Brucie B. His classic tape is in every true hip-hop immortal's crib getting continuous play. These are my dogs and broads who I admire and respect. They've become great in our ears by cuttin' and tearin' other people's records. They found themes for the huge steps hip-hop has taken in our lives. On a forty million dollar picture, you'll hear Gary Newman's films (an old school classic) getting edited from the 33 & 1/3 generation tape in Heavy D's trailer. Snoop plays the break beat "Action" in his headphones while he sits on the set and John Singleton amps "Take The Money And Run" in his Lincoln Navigator. Cut to: Nike's "Freestyle Sounds of Basketball" which is actually "Planet Rock" (created by Afrika Bambaataa). It's SHAZAMBO! That means that

it's the perfect example of hip-hop's immortality within the world of capitalism and the dopest commercial Nike has ever made. No matter what song turns you on, make your personal anthem the same as ours: Cheryl Lynn's "Got To Be Real." This will keep both the blockparties and this book in ya heart, until we meet again in the park! The agency wanted a break of pace, so for the sake of space, we voted to let their pictures speak a thousand words; one for each of the present and future musicians they've touched. For their undying luv, and strenuous effort to the cultural enhancement, please join us in waving our hands from side to side by turning these pages. Respect, collect, and protect other people's recordz.

CONCEPT PRODUCTION PUBLISHER

MATTHEW SUROFF DEREK AXELROD MARK SUROFF PONTI LAMBROS

www.sockbandit.com
www.hiphopimmortals.com
www.wegotyourkids.com
1-877-IMMORTAL

ART DIRECTION & DESIGN BY No11
www.no11.com
Giovanni C. Russo/Art Direction & Design
Jesse Shadoan/Graphic Design
Pace Kaminsky/Graphic Design

WRITTEN BY
Bonz Malone
For Sock Bandit Productions

EDITED BY
Nichole Beattie
For Sock Bandit Productions

CONTRIBUTING EDITOR
DJ Lindy

CONTRIBUTING PRODUCERS
Michael Lindenbaum & Michael Rapaport

PHOTO EDITORS
Sock Bandit Productions
No11

PHOTOGRAPHER RELATIONS
Sock Bandit Productions
No11
Candice Marks
Piotr Sikora
Elizabeth Bruneau

ARTIST RELATIONS
Doug E. Fresh
Kelly Jackson
Terrance Colter

NAVIGATOR
Greg della Stua

Prepress
All prepress services and Direct To Plate File Preparation
for offshore productions:
Jaguar Advanced Graphics
www.jaguargraphics.com
New York
DG,CG,VS,RL

INTERNATIONAL RELATIONS
Ponti Lambros & Candice Marks

DIRECTOR OF VIDEO & FILM PRODUCTION
Kris Palestrini

PHOTOGRAPHIC RETOUCHING SERVICES
Piotr Pixelman Bondarczyk & Joanna Holuj

PHOTOGRAPHIC REPRODUCTION SERVICES
Black + White and Color Edge
Chelsea Black & White

ACKNOWLEDGMENTS

We would like to offer our sincere Thanks to: All whose efforts helped make this happen.

All of the artists that grace the pages of this amazing book.

All the gifted Photographers and their people that helped make this a reality, without your hard work none of this would have been possible:
Annalisa, Jerome Albertini, Armen, Janette Beckman, Teri Bloom, Raymond Boyd, Chris Buck, Danny Clinch, Michel Comte, David Corio, Matthew Dean, Peter Dokus, Sante D'Orazio, George DuBose, Roger Erickson, Jesse Frohman, Marc Hom, T. Hopkins, Gregory Jackson, Hassan Jarane, Eric Johnson, Jeffrey Kane, David Katzenstein, Kevin Knight, David LaChapelle, Christian Lantry, Michael Lavine, Robert Lewis, Dana Lixenberg, Anthony Mandler, Clay Patrick McBride, Mark Mann, Jonathan Mannion, Estevan Oriol, Ernie Paniccioli, Ebet Roberts, Matthew Salacuse, Mike Schreiber, Mark Seliger, Ivory Serra, Jamel Shabazz, Piotr Sikora, Atsuko Tanaka, Max Vadukul, Nitin Vadukul, Ceza Vera, Christian Witkin.

All the artists and their management who gave us the time to shoot them exclusively for Hip Hop Immortals Vol.1 The Remix:
Snoop, Xzibit, The Roots, Stetsasonic, DJ Quik, Battle Cat, Too Short, Domino.

Giovanni, your hard work and commitment on such an unpredictable project brought our ideas to life.

Release Entertainment, Mike Rapaport and Michael Lindemnbaum for being there all the time.

Bonz Malone and Nichole Beattie and Dj Lindy. The words were a major part of this project.

Kris Palestrini for: Hip Hop Immortals We Got Your Kids

Raja and Jeffrey Kane @ Color Edge and Black + White and Vickie, Michael & Marion at Chelsea Black and White.

Our Friends, Families and everyone else who played such a critical role in making Hip Hop Immortals Vol 1 a reality: An overwhelming Thanks to:
TS and Big Len, MA & DA, Slate, Bobbie, Paige Axelrod, Michael Axelrod, Joan Axelrod, Kim Sozzi, NikeTown, P1 & fam, P2, Uncle T & 19 Street Gym, Aaron Simon, Racer & D, Zach & Lana, Chuckey, Big Jay, Rasheeda @ Color Edge, Fred & Darbin@Fotocare, Warren Sapp, Doug E. Fresh, Steve Yano, Rob P & Nikki at Scratch Media, Flava Jay & Q + all of KC, Pace Kaminsky, Carrie Hunt, Jesse Shadoan, Cheri McGee, Christian Towner, Jordon Weiss, Kelly Jackson, Sway, Josh Behar, Doug Davis, Steven Kaplan, Rob Weinstein, Manie Barrow, Claudine Arthurs, Dave Kelly /London Features, Mr. Kinky, Jon Cohen/Cornerstone, Kris Palestrini, Jamallie Bradley, Lou Marinelli, Ted Franklin, Regina Ang, Alan Adelson, Yevette Overton, Cliff Feldstein, Norm Maxwell, Tami P., Brad Swonetz, Greg Gurusso, David Senatra, Joe Burke, Aaron Stone, Steve Powers, Jesse Itzler, Terrance Colter, Johnny Limo, Johnny Jump, Sparks Steakhouse, Roberta @ Nava, Jamel Shabazz, Gregory Johnson, Jeff Sledge @ Jive Records, Modesto, "Big"Colin Mcnish/c-money, Jamie & Anita @ Patrick Mcmullen, Jen Factor, Maureen Bray, Alan@PBI, Matt Marcus, Master Coug, Peaches, Frankie Favors, Zoo Dog and fam., Hanos, Alwex H,K,J, ASW, M. Levin, Sammy w, Al & Vin, Andy & P Fam. AAA,, Asbert, Bonz Malone, The coach , C& D Goldberg, Bot, Yoon, Burton, M Rose, Breathless Destination , Matt Cat., Caribbean Dream, Rick& Barbara, Danzig Fam, Dirty, EPMD, Bum, J. Minnesota, J&R Castello, Kenny F., Mike I ,Leo, Aldo & Gregg ,Coco, Pen, Pachino, Newton, Mr. & Mrs. Kim, Saluzzi, Shalva, Manny Simon, Walter V., D-Money, 3Zeebras, Randy Z., Gui, Woody, Cathyann, Scot Rosenberg, The Zell Fam., Meri G., Rich Abend, Pete Santinello, Krav Maga inc., Venesio Wear, Buddha, Bum, Jason & Noah, Strategic Group, Tucker & fam., Michael Rapaport, Michael Lindenbaum, Release Ent., Big Mike the bodyguard, Nichole Beattie, Greg della Stua, Candice Marks, Art Partners, Lawrence Hayle, John Kochanski, Mike Peredo, Paul Joseph, Adam Port, Darren S., SJ, Elizabeth Bruneau, Lisa @ Danny Clinch, Dawn @ Christian Witkin, Amy @ Michael Lavine, Alexis @Jonathon Mannion, Shelter @Mark Seliger, Sandy @DavidLaChapelle, Stella, Johnny Nunez, Benny ICE, Command Pr Jonathan Cheban, Stacey Wechsler, Ponti Lambros, Daniel Tam, Caroline, Christina, Eric Poppleton, Bruce Hubco, Mapplethorpe Studios, BM, The Mates, Darren Shneider, Paul Kerzner, Paul Richards, Andrew Meltzer, Brad Leffe, Bennett Orfaly, P3, Dan & Michael@Avalon Publishing, Lana@SAStudio, Mr. Cartoon, Mariana Vadukul, Sarah Marusek@smpublicrelations. M.L.L., Steve Rifkind, Gabey, Pete Blast, Mikey B., Groovey Lou, Echo Hattix, Jen Allison, Estevan Oriol, Neil Ortenberg

And to all those who we missed.

A portion of the proceeds from Hip Hop Immortals Volume One and other services will be donated to a variety of charitable organizations.

PEACE TO ALL THE FALLEN:

JAM MASTER JAY

AALIYAH

EAZY E

BIG L

BIG PUN

NOTORIOUS B.I.G

2PAC

LISA "LEFT EYE" LOPES

9-11-01

THE WORLD WILL NEVER FORGET

HIP HOP IMMORTALS VOLUME 1 THE REMIX

Published by
Thunder's Mouth Press
An Imprint of Avalon Publishing Group Incorporated
161 William St., 16th Floor
New York, NY 10038

This book was printed without film at a 200 line screen, plates were imaged by Creo Lotem Quantum
Platesetter on 135gsm european gloss paper then section sewn with a laminated cardstock, cover drawn on.
Fonts used: No.11 Engravers, under the supervison of AmericanBook in Singapore.

Scanning, prepress services by Jaguar Advanced Graphics www.jaguargraphics.com

Library of Congress Cataloging-in-Publication Data is available.

ISBN: 1-56025-518-8

10 9 8 7 6 5 4 3 2 1

First Edition

Hip Hop Immortals Volume One was first published as a casebound 12" by 15 1/4" limited edition in 2002

Casebound book and Hip Hop Immortals Volume 1 The Remix are both designed by: Giovanni C. Russo/No.11

www.hiphopimmortals.com

Hip Hop Immortals is a trademark of Sock Bandit Productions, Inc.

Hip Hop Immortals Volume 1 The Remix is distributed by Publishers Group West

2 Pac
Danny Clinch *left*
David LaChapelle *right*
www.dannyclinch.com
www.davidlachapelle.com

House of Pain
Jesse Frohman
www.jessefrohman.com

IS SYNONYMOUS WITH THE SUMMER OF
1992 AND WITH NEARLY EVERY PARTY ANY-
ONE ATTENDED FOR THE NEXT
AROUND JUMP
PERSON LIVING IN THE UNITED STATES AND
BORN ON OR AFTER THE YEAR 1970

House of Pain
Estevan Oriol
www.estevanoriol.com

Snoop Dogg
Nitin Vadukul *left*
Christian Witkin *right*
www.nitinvadukul.com
www.christianwitkin.com

Snoop Dogg
Matthew Dean
matt@immortalbrands.com

Ludacris
Matthew Salacuse

The Roots & Stetsasonic
Danny Clinch
www.dannyclinch.com

The Roots & Stetsasonic
Matthew Dean
matt@immortalbrands.com

Left page
Janette Beckman
Annalisa
www.rapphotos.com

Right page
Ernie Paniccioli
Mark Seliger
www.proofphoto.com

Ultra Magnetic MC's
Anthony Mandler *left*
Michael Lavine *right*
www.michaellavine.com

Grand Master Caz
Ebet Roberts
www.ebetroberts.com

Grand Master Caz
Atsuko Tanaka
www.atsukotanaka.com

Whodini
Danny Clinch
www.dannyclinch.com

Eazy E
Peter Dokus
www.peterdokus.com

Wu-Tang Clan
Jerome Albertini
www.albertinistudio.net

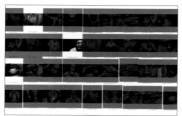

Wu-Tang Clan
Jerome Albertini
www.albertinistudio.net

Grandmaster Flash
Clay Patrick McBride
www.claypatrickmcbride.com

Grandmaster Flash
David Corio
www.davidcorio.com

Bones Thugs-N- Harmony
Roger Erickson
www.mercuryartistgroup.com

The Beatnuts
Piotr Sikora
www.piotrsikora.com

Afrika Bambaataa
Janette Beckman
www.janettebeckman.com

**Afrika Bambaataa
& The Soul Sonic Force**
George DuBose
www.george-dubose.com

Fat Boys
Ebet Roberts
www.ebetroberts.com

Salt-N-Pepa
Mark Seliger
www.proofphoto.com

Salt-N-Pepa
David Corio
www.davidcorio.com

Pete Rock & C.L. Smooth
Piotr Sikora
www.piotrsikora.com

Cold Crush Brothers
Joey Kane

Mc Hammer
Raymond Boyd
www.raymondboyd.com

Dj Jazzy Jeff & The Fresh Prince
David Corio
www.davidcorio.com

Rob Base
Janette Beckman
www.janettebeckman.com

Tone Loc
Janette Beckman
www.janettebeckman.com

Eve
Christian Witkin
www.christianwitkin.com

Eve
Marc Hom *left*
Eric Johnson *right*
www.artpartner.com
www.ericjohnsonphotography.com

Left page
David Katzenstein
Janette Beckman
www.davidkatzenstein.com
www.janettebeckman.com

Right page
George DuBose
Robert Lewis
www.george-dubose.com

Jay-z
Jonathan Mannion
www.jonathanmannion.com

Jay-z
Dana Lixenberg
www.zphotographic.com

Jay-z
Nitin Vadukul *left*
Jonathan Mannion *right*
www.nitinvadukul.com
www.jonathanmannion.com

So So Def

Jermaine Dupri
Jerome Albertini
www.albertinistudio.net

Doug E. Fresh
David Corio
www.davidcorio.com

Kool G Rap & D.J. Polo
George DuBose/ London Features
www.george-dubose.com

Too $hort
Jonathan Mannion
www.jonathanmannion.com

EMPD
Armen
www.armenexpo.com

Chubb Rock
Jesse Frohman
www.jessefrohman.com

A Tribe Called Quest
Mark Seliger *left*
Eric Johnson *right*
www.proofphoto.com
www.ericjohnsonphotography.com

Coolio
David LaChapelle
www.davidlachapelle.com

Coolio
David LaChapelle *left*
Annalisa *right*
www.davidlachapelle.com
www.annalisaphotography.com

Kool Moe Dee
Gregory Jackson
www.gregoryjacksonphotography.com

KRS-One/ BDP
Janette Beckman
www.janettebeckman.com

Public Enemy
Cesar Vera
www.CesarVera.com

Public Enemy
David Corio
www.davidcorio.com

Public Enemy
Jesse Frohman
www.jessefrohman.com

P.Diddy-Puffy Combs
Dana Lixenberg
www.zphotographic.com

P.Diddy-Puffy Combs
Michael Lavine
www.michaellavine.com

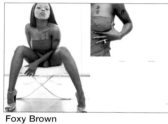

Foxy Brown
Christian Witkin
www.christianwitkin.com

The Furious Five
Janette Beckman
www.janettebeckman.com

The Fugees
Danny Clinch
www.dannyclinch.com

Heavy D
Sante D' Orazio
www.mercuryartistgroup.com

Ice-T
Mark Seliger
www.proofphoto.com

Ice-T
Mark Seliger
www.proofphoto.com

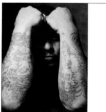

Kid Frost
Danny Clinch
www.dannyclinch.com

Ja Rule
Jonathan Mannion *left*
Nitin Vadukul *right*
www.jonathanmannion.com
www.nitinvadukul.com

Nelly
Jonathan Mannion
www.jonathanmannion.com

Lauryn Hill
Eric Johnson
www.ericjohnsonphotography.com

Ice Cube
Jesse Frohman
www.jessefrohman.com

DJ Quik
Roger Erickson
www.mercuryartistgroup.com

Graffiti Images
Courtesy of the writer's bench

Lil' Kim
David LaChapelle
www.davidlachapelle.com

Lil' Kim
Max Vadukul *left*
David LaChapelle *right*
www.artpartner.com
www.davidlachapelle.com

10 9 8 7 6 5 4 3 2 1

DJ and Producers:

Top row left to right

Kid Capri
Matthew Dean

DJ Brucie B
Erin Patrice O'brien
www.erinpatriceobrien.com

DJ Clue
Mo Daoud
www.modaoud.com

Battlecat
Roger Erickson

Lovebug Starski
Gregory Jackson

DJ Mark the 45 King
Ernie Paniccioli

Timbaland
Erin Patrice O'brien

Prince Paul
Mo Daoud
www.modaoud.com

Bottom row left to right

DJ Premier
Eric Johnson

DJ Polo
Jesse Frohman

DJ Red Alert
Jesse Frohman

Marley Marl
George DuBose/London Features

Funkmaster Flex
Mo Daoud
www.modaoud.com

RZA
Michael Lavine

Mr. Magic
Hassan Jarane

Domino
Matthew Dean

That is

book w

opened

expec

and

with pr

pr or

Alcott

That is a good book which is opened with expectation and closed with profit.   -A. Bronson Alcott

In closing, the life of a Hip-Hop Immortal does not exempt them from sin and imperfection or punishment as they live out their earthly existence. The idea of style and the rules of competing for the best one dictates that nothing is too small to know and nothing is too big to attempt. For the MC/Rapper, it's rocking the mic. For the B-Boys and B-Girls, you gotta rock your body and dance, and for Graffiti Writers, we go all-city to be kings by "bombing" the trains. To advance a sub-culture takes thousands of hours of practice before going IPO. Throughout the years of evolution, there have been countless internal wars fought over who should lead the movement. Hip-hop isn't a thing to be led! It's a culture and a culture is formed by process and that process is based on the evolution of its society, whether public or private. We are one body as a collective that cannot live without the four components kept in mind. There are few CEOs of rap, most of which have been rewarded for their consistency and dedication to improving on where others fell short. However, there is no CEO of hip-hop. There is a governing body that once wrote policy and they are immortalized as well, but the ones who were entrusted to lead after them fell victim to their own success. They wanted to be Demigods rather than, or shall I say, greater than demagogues. Like the ancient tales of Camelot, the round ideology had been abandoned and darkness fell upon the kingdom and rendered it powerless. Today, the only grail left to be found is balance. An elixir that must be poured out by a Demagogue with a principled message greater than a demigod's power. None of those who were there in the beginning will ever be defeated. They have no name that is of greater importance than the other, just a balanced view of Freedom, Justice, and Equality that inspired and empowered others, not pulled them apart. This is our universal nation that simple artisans of the out-class either yearn for its return to anonymity, or help divide our turf with bastars of rap's perverted and corruptive place in the General Market. Is this too much for y'all? Can you deal with it? If not, then don't bother writing anymore lyrics or putting strips of adhesive tape on records like *DJ Speedy the Cheat!* Don't pick up a marker or a can of krylon like you got a name somebody's supposed to care about, let alone remember some day when you're either dead or in jail! Don't lie to yourself thinking that there is a place for you in the pantheon of forthcoming pages, cause obviously, there's no room. Chairs are set for those who advance the art and enrich the culture. For the rest of the selfish, who are but dim-witted starz that fall by the dawns early light, it's standing room only. If you can't chew these fat pieces of sugarless gum, then there won't be another forward written on this subject. In order for the process of evolution to continue, this book must also become obsolete, written by those with full understanding and a deep insight of both past and future movements. A champion does not always take first place. There are those who win and are not respected. Herein lies the names of the immortals who have suffered loss gracefully, with dignity. For to these, the respect of their peers is worth as much as an undisputed victory. The youth of yesterday have grown to add on to the foundation that the kingdom and the power left in the dark for we are the Kids of Camelot. The children of the ghetto who crawled as wannabes, so we could one day wear the Wallabees. Whether great mind or gangster, this book is made of contributions given and taken away. We know the difference between Hip-Hop: the multi-cultural juggernaut created to stop gang violence through artist expression and solidarity, and Rap; the Jerry Heller, Helen Keller marriage that produces verbal abortions and then grows them in corporate daycare centers. We remember the brothers and young mothers who formed nursery rhymes that now make platinum memories. The ghetto's only superheroes loyally defending the round ideologyudice art form. No hip-hop immortal will ever ascend to true glory based on their monetary wealth. Their personal code of keeping it real violates the universal order to keep it round! They and all those to follow must prove beyond any universal shadow of a doubt that they have surpassed the introduction of knowledge of self and have publicly entered in the sacred realm of self-mastery! We are counting on you to take us on your continued journey. Guard your heart and we will be here with the force of a nation by your side. You know us when you hear us. One will scratch, the other will rhyme. In the pursuit of excellence there is no finish line. Just like 1979, there will be others who will make the summer shine and I'm proud of you.

Now, let's begin.

That is a good book which is opened with expectation and closed with profit.   -A. Bronson Alcott

In closing, the life of a Hip-Hop Immortal does not exempt them from sin and imperfection or punishment as they live out their earthly existence. The idea of style and the rules of competing for the best one dictates that nothing is too small to know and nothing is too big to attempt. For the MC/Rapper, it's rocking the mic. For the B-Boys and B-Girls, you gotta rock your body and dance, and for Graffiti Writers, we go all-city to be kings by "bombing" the trains. To advance a sub-culture takes thousands of hours of practice before going IPO. Throughout the years of evolution, there have been countless internal wars fought over who should lead the movement. Hip-hop isn't a thing to be led! It's a culture and a culture is formed by process and that process is based on the evolution of its society, whether public or private. We are one body as a collective that cannot live without the four components kept in mind. There are few CEOs of rap, most of which have been rewarded for their consistency and dedication to improving on where others fell short. However, there is no CEO of hip-hop. There is a governing body that once wrote policy and they are immortalized as well, but the ones who were entrusted to lead after them fell victim to their own success. They wanted to be Demigods rather than, or shall I say, greater than demagogues. Like the ancient tales of Camelot, the round ideology had been abandoned and darkness fell upon the kingdom and rendered it powerless. Today, the only grail left to be found is balance. An elixir that must be poured out by a Demagogue with a principled message greater than a demigod's power. None of those who were there in the beginning will ever be defeated. They have no name that is of greater importance than the other, just a balanced view of Freedom, Justice, and Equality that inspired and empowered others, not pulled them apart. This is our universal nation that simple artisans of the out-class either yearn for its return to anonymity, or help divide our turf with bastars of rap's perverted and corruptive place in the General Market. Is this too much for y'all? Can you deal with it? If not, then don't bother writing anymore lyrics or putting strips of adhesive tape on records like *DJ Speedy the Cheat!* Don't pick up a marker or a can of krylon like you got a name somebody's supposed to care about, let alone remember some day when you're either dead or in jail! Don't lie to yourself thinking that there is a place for you in the pantheon of forthcoming pages, cause obviously, there's no room. Chairs are set for those who advance the art and enrich the culture. For the rest of the selfish, who are but dim-witted starz that fall by the dawns early light, it's standing room only. If you can't chew these fat pieces of sugarless gum, then there won't be another forward written on this subject. In order for the process of evolution to continue, this book must also become obsolete, written by those with full understanding and a deep insight of both past and future movements. A champion does not always take first place. There are those who win and are not respected. Herein lies the names of the immortals who have suffered loss gracefully, with dignity. For to these, the respect of their peers is worth as much as an undisputed victory. The youth of yesterday have grown to add on to the foundation that the kingdom and the power left in the dark for we are the Kids of Camelot. The children of the ghetto who crawled as wannabes, so we could one day wear the Wallabees. Whether great mind or gangster, this book is made of contributions given and taken away. We know the difference between Hip-Hop: the multi-cultural juggernaut created to stop gang violence through artist expression and solidarity, and Rap; the Jerry Heller, Helen Keller marriage that produces verbal abortions and then grows them in corporate daycare centers. We remember the brothers and young mothers who formed nursery rhymes that now make platinum memories. The ghetto's only superheroes loyally defending the round ideologyudice art form. No hip-hop immortal will ever ascend to true glory based on their monetary wealth. Their personal code of keeping it real violates the universal order to keep it round! They and all those to follow must prove beyond any universal shadow of a doubt that they have surpassed the introduction of knowledge of self and have publicly entered in the sacred realm of self-mastery! We are counting on you to take us on your continued journey. Guard your heart and we will be here with the force of a nation by your side. You know us when you hear us. One will scratch, the other will rhyme. In the pursuit of excellence there is no finish line. Just like 1979, there will be others who will make the summer shine and I'm proud of you.

Now, let's begin.

That is a good book which is opened with expectation and closed with profit.   -A. Bronson Alcott

In closing, the life of a Hip-Hop Immortal does not exempt them from sin and imperfection or punishment as they live out their earthly existence. The idea of style and the rules of competing for the best one dictates that nothing is too small to know and nothing is too big to attempt. For the MC/Rapper, it's rocking the mic. For the B-Boys and B-Girls, you gotta rock your body and dance, and for Graffiti Writers, we go all-city to be kings by "bombing" the trains. To advance a sub-culture takes thousands of hours of practice before going IPO. Throughout the years of evolution, there have been countless internal wars fought over who should lead the movement. Hip-hop isn't a thing to be led! It's a culture and a culture is formed by process and that process is based on the evolution of its society, whether public or private. We are one body as a collective that cannot live without the four components kept in mind. There are few CEOs of rap, most of which have been rewarded for their consistency and dedication to improving on where others fell short. However, there is no CEO of hip-hop. There is a governing body that once wrote policy and they are immortalized as well, but the ones who were entrusted to lead after them fell victim to their own success. They wanted to be Demigods rather than, or shall I say, greater than demagogues. Like the ancient tales of Camelot, the round ideology had been abandoned and darkness fell upon the kingdom and rendered it powerless. Today, the only grail left to be found is balance. An elixir that must be poured out by a Demagogue with a principled message greater than a demigod's power. None of those who were there in the beginning will ever be defeated. They have no name that is of greater importance than the other, just a balanced view of Freedom, Justice, and Equality that inspired and empowered others, not pulled them apart. This is our universal nation that simple artisans of the out-class either yearn for it's return to anonymity, or help divide our turf with bastars of rap's perverted and corruptive place in the General Market. Is this too much for y'all? Can you deal with it? If not, then don't bother writing anymore lyrics or putting strips of adhesive tape on records like *DJ Speedy the Cheat!* Don't pick up a marker or a can of krylon like you got a name somebody's supposed to care about, let alone remember some day when you're either dead or in jail! Don't lie to yourself thinking that there is a place for you in the pantheon of forthcoming pages, cause obviously, there's no room. Chairs are set for those who advance the art and enrich the culture. For the rest of the selfish, who are but dim-witted starz that fall by the dawns early light, it's standing room only. If you can't chew these fat pieces of sugarless gum, then there won't be another forward written on this subject. In order for the process of evolution to continue, this book must also become obsolete, written by those with full understanding and a deep insight of both past and future movements. A champion does not always take first place. There are those who win and are not respected. Herein lies the names of the immortals who have suffered loss gracefully, with dignity. For to these, the respect of their peers is worth as much as an undisputed victory. The youth of yesterday have grown to add on to the foundation that the kingdom and the power left in the dark for we are the Kids of Camelot. The children of the ghetto who crawled as wannabes, so we could one day wear the Wallabees. Whether great mind or gangster, this book is made of contributions given and taken away. We know the difference between Hip-Hop: the multi-cultural juggernaut created to stop gang violence through artist expression and solidarity, and Rap; the Jerry Heller, Helen Keller marriage that produces verbal abortions and then grows them in corporate daycare centers. We remember the brothers and young mothers who formed nursery rhymes that now make platinum memories. The ghetto's only superheroes loyally defending the round ideologyudice art form. No hip-hop immortal will ever ascend to true glory based on their monetary wealth. Their personal code of keeping it real violates the universal order to keep it round! They and all those to follow must prove beyond any universal shadow of a doubt that they have surpassed the introduction of knowledge of self and have publicly entered in the sacred realm of self-mastery! We are counting on you to take us on your continued journey. Guard your heart and we will be here with the force of a nation by your side. You know us when you hear us. One will scratch, the other will rhyme. In the pursuit of excellence there is no finish line. Just like 1979, there will be others